A Young Man's
Dream

A Young Man's
Dream

AN OLD MAN'S REALITY

WYVEDA I. PHILBERT

ARPress
ILLUMINATING IDEAS
EMPOWERING VOICES

ARPress
45 Dan Road Suite 5
Canton, MA 02021

Hotline: 1(888) 821-0229
Fax: 1(508) 545-7580

Ordering Information:
Quantity sales. Special discounts are available on quantity purchases by corporations,associations, and others. For details, contact the publisher at the address above.

Printed in the United States of America.

ISBN-13: Softcover 979-8-89330-870-9
eBook 979-8-89330-871-6

Library of Congress Control Number: 2024901776

TABLE OF CONTENTS

DEDICATED

To my husband, Joe, who had the determination
to carry out his boyhood dream.

And to my dear friend, Dee, who gave me the
courage to go with him.

A special thank you to Ruth for all her
help and encouragement.

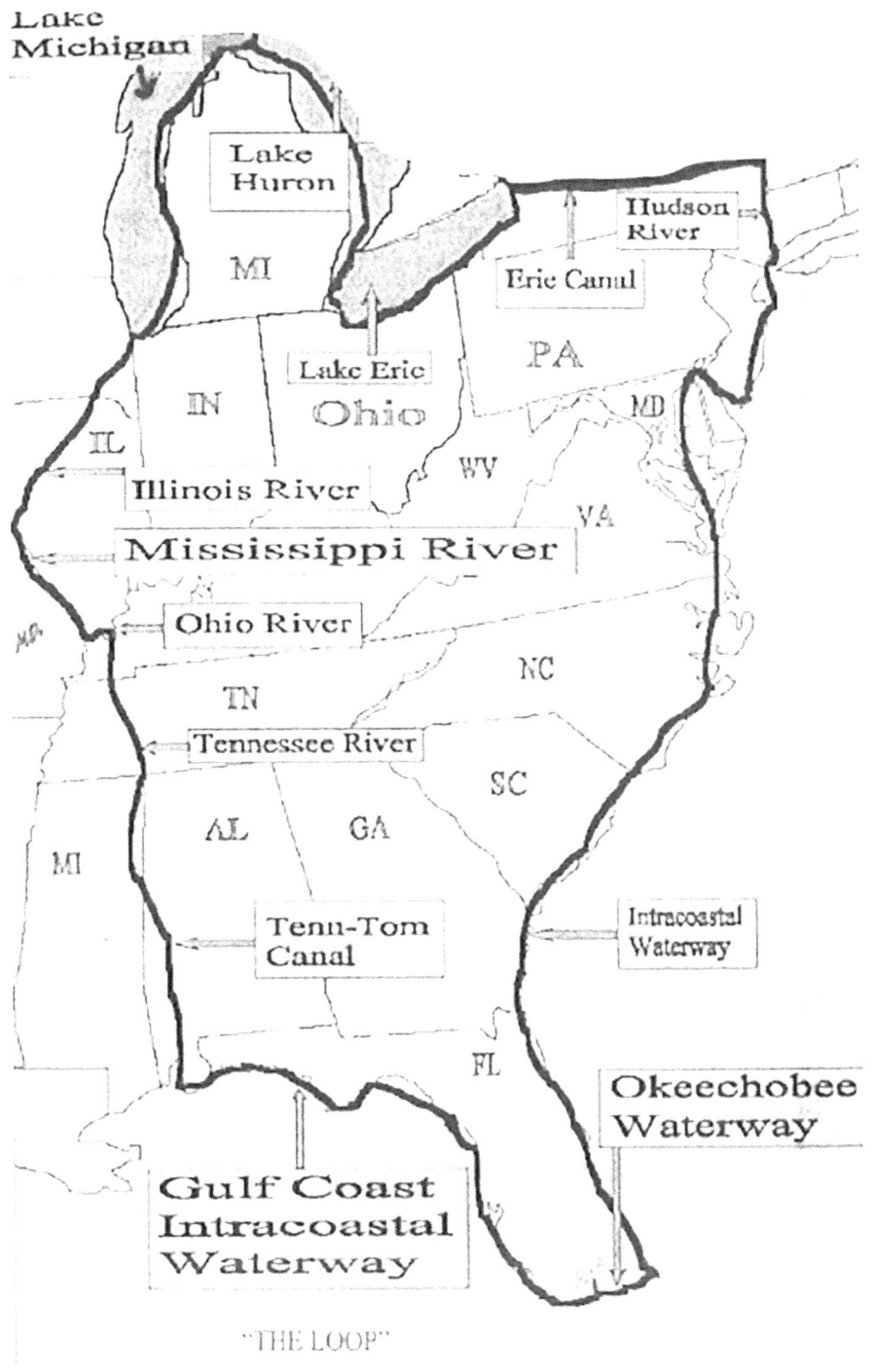

Lake Michigan

Lake Huron

MI

Lake Erie

Hudson River

Eric Canal

PA

IN

Ohio

MD

IL

Illinois River

WV

VA

Mississippi River

Ohio River

MO

NC

TN

Tennessee River

SC

AL

GA

MI

Tenn-Tom Canal

Intracoastal Waterway

FL

Okeechobee Waterway

Gulf Coast Intracoastal Waterway

"THE LOOP"

v

INTRODUCTION

Ever since he was a teenager, a young man named Joe dreamed of taking the boat trip called The Loop, or The Great Circle. After reading an article about Ann Davidson, who had made the trip solo on a 17-foot outboard cruiser back in the 1950's, he was determined that someday he would also make that same trip. He even built a small boat while in high school, so he has had the bug for quite a while. In fact, when we got married, Joe told me about this dream. I said, "Sure, I'll go," not thinking he would ever do it. I was never around boats or water and didn't even have a clue what he was really talking about. I can't even swim!

After he retired in 1996, we bought a 31-foot sailboat specifically to make this trip. It needed a little work done to it, and Joe wanted to go over the engine compartment, making an overall inspection to make sure it was seaworthy. We worked on it for the next five years while living on it during the winter months in Florida with our cat "Cotton."

All this time, I was thinking I'm not going on a six-month boat trip. Someone has to stay back in Indiana to take care of our 90-acre farm. I thought that I would stay in Indiana and he would find someone to go with him. He found several people who wanted to go with him, but either work and/or lack of money wouldn't allow them the opportunity.

While in Florida prior to the year he was planning to take the trip, he told everyone about it and that I wasn't going with him. Some thought he was crazy; some thought I was crazy. The couples that had made the trip told me I should go and they couldn't understand why I didn't want to go. Of course, I told them about the farm and all my other excuses, but they didn't even hesitate when they said "Go." It would be a wonderful adventure of a lifetime. They told me about the many historical places and wildlife to be seen along the canals and rivers. Some had made the trip twice and were trying to figure out how to go again. They said that something new could be seen on each trip. But, living six months on a boat?

Many travel by boat down the east coast every year to winter in Florida, but they don't do the Loop. However, many dream of doing the Loop but never get to do so. And here I have the opportunity right in front of me.

Joe was going to make the trip with or without help. Being red and green colorblind, he knew he would be at a disadvantage because the navigational markers are red and green. A second strike against him was being 65 years old and having high blood pressure. A third strike was whether he would be able to obtain his medication along the way.

My brother wanted to go but couldn't figure out how to get someone to run his business for six months. He finally said he would take off and go because it was a chance of a lifetime for him also. It was all planned for the spring of 2003 when Joe and my brother would sail the Loop.

Then Fate dealt her hand. While living on the boat at our dock in Alva, we needed to fill the water tank. We decided to take it down the Okeechobee Waterway to the Franklin Locks and campground that is run by the Army Corps of Engineers. We would stay for a few days, fill up with water, and then take it back to our dock in Alva.

Usually boat people don't have any transportation, but we had brought our truck so we could get into town. Early one morning, literally by accident, we met this couple from Virginia, Rodger and Dee.

They came over to our boat, and Rodger told us his wife had cut her two middle fingers with a knife the night before while slicing bread. She needed to get to the emergency room. Joe was taking the keys out of his pocket as Rodger was speaking; he scolded them for not coming over the night before. He told them to take the truck, gave directions to the local hospital, and said to take all the time they needed and not worry about anything here.

Later that afternoon they returned and reported she had severed the tendons on her two fingers and was going to need surgery and several weeks of therapy. Since you can stay at these locks for only three weeks (it's meant to be a stopover for people traveling through), Rodger and Dee would have to find another place for their boat, and most marinas are full this time of the year. We took them to see our friend Ernie who owns the marina where we usually stay. Being the nice man that he is, he was able to help them.

The year before, it was so cold here in Florida that we were freezing on the boat. We bought a condo, which happens to be on Palm Beach Boulevard across from Ernie's marina. We were in a convenient place to be able to help them with transportation. They did end up getting a rental car so they could run their errands, but they could have used our truck. We ended up going out to eat and running around together, becoming really good friends. Actually, I think it was friendship at first sight.

Now, getting back to the Loop, it turned out that my brother couldn't get away from his defense business (bad timing with the war). Joe was going with or without my help. My gut feeling was he couldn't do it alone. Even though he had read and studied many books and articles, he still didn't know what actually was ahead of him. Would he stay healthy? Could he deal with the navigational markers that are key to staying in the channels?

Rodger and Dee were headed back home to Virginia when the accident happened. Since they were so late getting started back, they talked me into going up the east coast as far as Virginia, getting off with them, and catching a ride back home to Indiana. We could follow them and see how we liked traveling the waterway. Knowing I would feel better traveling with another couple that had already done some boat traveling on the ICW, I decided to be more open-minded about the trip. I agreed to go as far as Virginia. We did have a lot of fun together, and they are a super nice couple.

I thought by going as far as Virginia I could see whether Joe could handle things by himself. I would make up my mind whether or not to go the whole distance by the time we got there. I knew there was a big chance I might have to go all the way, but I had about six weeks to make up my mind one way or the other.

There were a few people who didn't think Joe would ever make this trip or that I would ever consider going with him at all. So the big question is . . .

Did I jump off in Virginia or did I go the distance and make The Great Circle?

CHAPTER 1
SOUTH - EAST:
ALVA FLORIDA- - -REEDVILLE , VIRGINIA

Saturday, April 19, 2003

We left our dock in Alva, Florida, on a beautiful sunny morning on our 31-foot Bombay Clipper pilothouse sailboat (without her mast) named "Whoosher." We met our friends Rodger and Dee on their 36-foot Gulfstar trawler they call "Pockets." We came from our canal and met them out in the Okeechobee Waterway, once a major transportation artery during the settling of Florida. It is still a beautiful waterway in a straight route across the state.

"Whoosher" was loaded down with supplies and, with the American flag hanging off her stern, was ready to make The Loop, or The Great Circle. This is a 5,000-mile (or more) adventure mostly in protected waters called the Intracoastal Waterway, or ICW, going up the east coast, across the Erie Canal, through the Great Lakes, down the river system to Mobile, Alabama, across the Gulf of Mexico, down the west coast of Florida back to the Caloosahatchee River, making a circle back to your starting point. You can take as long as you want and start from any point, but you should be starting south from the upper peninsula of Michigan by August 25 or you could run into adverse conditions. Be sure to take along a heater of some sort; we left ours behind thinking we wouldn't need it (wrong).

"Pockets" is only going as far as the Chesapeake Bay off the coast of Virginia where she has a dock.

Meeting up with our friends at 7:15 a.m., we led the way going up the river and under the bascule bridge at Alva. A bascule bridge is a structure one end of which is counterbalanced by the other on the principle of a seesaw or by weights. It opens up to let boats go through that are too tall to pass under the bridge.

Joe's sister Mary and her husband Gregg live right on the river past the bridge at Alva. They were out on their front porch waving and yelling "Bon Voyage" and "God's Speed" as we started our journey. Rodger and Dee took the lead as we started the first day of our adventure.

We are on our way in Whoosher on the
Caloosahatchee starting the young man's dream.

We had a perfect day to start this adventure called the Great Circle, anchoring at 2:45 p.m. on the lakeside of the Moore Haven Lock, which is located on the north side of Okeechobee waterway. Moore Haven is well known as the center for the sugar cane industry.

After anchoring, Rodger and Dee paddled over in their dinghy to have a celebration toast, talk about the day, and decide tomorrow's destination.

Today was a good day; we traveled 33.3 nautical miles.

Easter Sunday, April 20, 2003

We pulled anchor at 7:15. Enjoying this beautiful Sunday morning after going through the locks yesterday at Moore Haven, we took the rim route around Lake Okeechobee. We decided last evening to go around the perimeter of the lake rather than across the middle. The outside route is 10 miles longer, but it's the more scenic, interesting alternative. Pelicans, egrets of all colors and sizes, and eagles are found here. The great bass fishing here should not be forgotten!

Every now and then we could look through the trees and see the lake. Lake Okeechobee is the second largest freshwater lake in the continental United States (after Lake Michigan). It has been likened to a saucer full of water, which is a good description because it is so shallow with depths from 11 to 17 feet, depending on the season. In strong winds the lake can become very choppy and turbulent in a short time, which is typical of shallow water. The lake is completely enclosed by an impressive levee system, and the aqua blue color of the water is spectacular.

We anchored at 3:15 p.m. inside Port Mayaca located on the east side of the lake. The locks serve as the entrance to the lake from the east. Numerous large alligators have been seen lurking in here, so no swimming or wading is allowed.

We had another good day on the water going 44.1 nautical miles.

Monday, April 21, 2003

We pulled up the anchor at 7:15 a.m. Heading east, we had to wait to go through the Saint Lucie lock. This is the first lock of the system that lifts or lowers. A lock has huge cement walls on both sides with gates at both ends. Water levels are raised or lowered and the gates at both ends close once you get inside. Then they let out the water or fill up the enclosure as you go from level to level on the water. This controls the water levels and helps prevent flooding. We were lowered approximately 13 feet. When approaching the lock, you either blow your air horn or call the lockmaster from the marine radio to request going through. Manatees sometimes lock through with you, making it necessary to take extra care going through this area. The locks here help control the water flow from Saint Lucie Canal to the Atlantic Ocean.

The canal is beautiful. We saw many kinds of birds feeding or perching in the trees along the waterway. I was always looking up at the trees or at the shore so I wouldn't miss anything.

We anchored at 2:15 p.m. in an inlet called Manatee Pocket off the ICW by Stuart, Florida. After securing the boat in the anchorage, Rodger and Dee rowed over in their dinghy with snacks and drinks to discuss the day, to see how we were doing so far, and to make plans for the next few days' journey. We enjoy just talking over the day with each other. So far, I'm glad I came; we are having very enjoyable and interesting days. We traveled 34.1 nautical miles today.

Tuesday, April 22, 2003

We pulled anchor at 7:10 a.m. and started up the ICW (Inter Coastal Waterway) in the Indian River. Porpoises played around us all afternoon. I could hear them blowing through their air holes, but finding them fast enough to get a picture with the camera was tricky. This was quite a sight to see them in the wild coming up beside our boat.

We anchored at 1:45 p.m. behind a little island called Jones Fruit Dock (but no fruit) where we were entertained with more porpoises playing and racing through the water past the boats. They were quite entertaining.

After settling in, Dee rowed over in the dinghy. I climbed down into the little inflatable, and we went fishing behind the boats with two sticks for fishing poles and a can of corn for bait. Believe it or not, we caught two catfish that were big enough to keep, but the guys didn't want to clean them so we turned them loose. We had a lot of fun, and of course no one thought we would catch anything.

This was another good day.

We traveled 37.8 nautical miles today.

Wednesday, April 23, 2003

We pulled up the anchor at 7:00 a.m. after enjoying our morning coffee. Every evening we decided on the starting time and about how many miles we would travel the next day. We radioed over to "Pockets" to exchange "good mornings" and headed out of the anchorage going north up the ICW past Sebastian and Melbourne. We stopped at Cocoa, Florida, where we strolled through the little restored town with its scenic murals painted on the sides of buildings, beautifully landscaped plazas, antique stores, art galleries, boutiques, and many restaurants. I wish we had gotten there earlier to go through some of the stores. Everything was closed except the restaurants. We finally decided on a restaurant called Murdock's where we all had a beer, ordered dinner, and talked and laughed. We had such a great time! But we always have a great time with Rodger and Dee; they are such a fun couple.

We walked back to our boats hand in hand to plan tomorrow and the next few days. Rodger is a good planner.

We traveled 42.4 nautical miles today.

Thursday, April 24, 2003

After leaving the marina at 7:00 a.m., we were back into the ICW heading north past Titusville where we could see Cape Canaveral off in the distance to the east. We passed the Kennedy Space Center, where

5

we could see space ships on display. There were tugboats pushing barges everywhere, making you wonder where they were headed with all the cargo they were pushing. The tugs really churned up the water, and you could feel it for several miles.

We headed up the ICW to the Haulover Canal, which is a mile-long cut that provides passage to the Indian River. The Indian fruit that you find in the grocery stores is grown here. Wildlife abounds through here, including pink flamingos. We were lucky enough to pass an island covered with flamingos, some feeding and some flying off to our port side (left). I wish we could have gone closer to the island to get a better look at them, but the water was too shallow around it.

There were so many different sizes and colors of herons and egrets on the waterway. An alligator was sunning himself on the bank. Rodger even saw a deer on shore and radioed back to us, but we missed seeing it. Deer don't usually stay around for sightseers. Gorgeous tall, graceful Australian pines with long-needled branches lined the shores of the channel, making an impressive sight.

We tried to stay in the channel where we had an eight-foot depth most of the time. Therefore, we had to keep a close eye on the depth meter because the wind can raise or lower the depth by two feet very quickly. We have a four-foot draft on our boat so we need at least that much water at all times.

Going through Mosquito Lagoon, another shallow expanse of water, we saw fishermen out, hoping to catch their share. From here we headed to New Smyrna, Florida, and anchored for the night in Sheephead Cut, which has nothing to do with sheep!

The wind and waves were so strong today. Joe really had to keep a strong hold on the wheel, which made for a tiring day. We were all ready to stop and throw out the anchor for the night.

We anchored in front of some condos. While sitting out in the cockpit relaxing, we noticed some round things about five inches in diameter floating past with the current. Being curious, Joe got the net out of the wet locker and pulled one out of the water. It was a jellyfish. Joe said it was actually heavy because it was full of water. It looked like a water balloon. There were hundreds of these beautiful maroon-and-cream-colored jellyfish floating past us in the swift current.

We had a nice relaxing evening.

We traveled 46.4 nautical miles.

Friday, April 25, 2003

We pulled the anchor at 7:00 a.m. on a cloudy day with a chance of rain and thunderstorms. Having had a few sprinkles already this morning and with a humid 85 degrees, we knew conditions were perfect for a storm.

We passed some impressive, absolutely gorgeous homes while going through Daytona, Ormond by the Sea, and Flagler Beach. They were as large as hotels and had picture-perfect landscaped lawns.

At 12:30 p.m. we pulled back into an unused channel that Rodger knew about because the weather was becoming very threatening. An old abandoned cement plant and a Sea Ray boat assembly plant are located there. This was a really nice, quiet anchorage back off the main channel. It provided protection from the storm that could hit us at any minute.

Dee had called on the marine radio earlier to invite us over for a spaghetti dinner on "Pockets," so Rodger rowed over in the dinghy to get us. It's a little tricky getting into a raft from the back of a sailboat, but where there's a will there's a way—even though it's not always pretty!

We had a delicious meal and were enjoying the evening when the wind started picking up. We decided we should get back to "Whoosher" while Rodger could still get back to his boat safely. It was starting to rain and the wind was getting really strong. We listened to the marine radio, which gave predictions of 70 mph winds. We were glad to be back in this little cove.

The sky was looking really nasty. While we were looking out the window, we saw the wind rip a piece of material off the bimini of "Pockets."

The next morning, while getting out to see how we were all doing after the windstorm, Rodger and Dee discovered their damage. They had to take down the bimini and steer from inside the boat until they could get it fixed. Steering from the fly bridge gives a much better view of the water. Without the bimini it gets really hot sitting there in the direct sun. The bimini is like an umbrella over your head protecting you from the sun.

We were very lucky today. You must always listen to the marine radio station and stay on top of weather conditions so you don't get caught out on the water in a storm. It was a wise decision going back in the cove for protection from the wind. Otherwise, it could have been a lot worse. Thanks to Rodger, we had a safe anchorage for the night.

Saturday, April 26, 2003

Pulling anchor again at 7:00 a.m., we headed up the river toward Saint Augustine, Florida. We stopped at the Hammonds Marina because "Pockets" needed fuel, and this marina had the best price on the waterway at $1.34 per gallon for diesel. We were a little early and had to wait for them to open.

Walking through the woods to a handy-mart for ice, we could hear peacocks but couldn't see them. When we got back to the fuel dock, we asked the dockworker about it. He said the woods were full of them, but only one had come out to visit; they had named him Homer. Peacocks are certainly noisy birds but are so very beautiful with those elongated tail feathers of iridescent colors.

"Pockets" now had fuel (about 200 gallons), and we headed north again on the ICW making The Great Circle.

There are more mansions along the waterway coming into Saint Augustine. On the right bank we saw a very tall white cross and then the fort, Castillo de San Marcos, a Spanish fort from the 1600's. There are traces of the Spanish military and their heritage everywhere through here.

Appearing on shore through the trees, the twin spires of a Catholic cathedral make an interesting skyline. All the history and historic landmarks through here make you wish you had the time to stop and go ashore to see it all. Anyone making a trip like this should schedule time to make some stops in some of the towns.

We went under a beautiful bridge called the Bridge of Lions, one of the most attractive bridges on the ICW. This is a double bascule bridge completed in 1928.

We docked in Saint Augustine off the San Sebastian River at the Oyster Creek Marina. We saw two eagles on a sandbar while sailing into the marina, and again there were porpoises all around us. Rodger's brother Denny drove down from Gainesville to usher us around so we could shop and pick up supplies. Rodger and Dee really lucked out by finding someone to fix the bimini by tomorrow.

Dee and I went to take our showers. Returning to the boat, we found our husbands and our boat neighbors having a party in the cockpit of "Whoosher," talking about the day's experiences, and telling stories of their travels. You get some interesting stories from boat captains (even a few tall tales).

One captain named Charlie Hall, who owned the big cruiser across the dock from us, had a cat named Pocko on board. Of course, I had to go over to talk to Pocko because I missed my cat. Everywhere we go, everyone loves our little boat "Whoosher"; so I gave them the five-minute tour and Joe answered all their questions.

After everyone returned to their own boats, the five of us walked from the marina to the local restaurant called Eddie's Oyster Bar. If you are ever in this area, you must eat at Eddie's. The food was so good—all-you-can-eat fish, shrimp, fries, hush puppies, and delicious iced tea. We were all so stuffed we could hardly walk back to our boats!

It was so nice of Denny to come down to drive us around. He is a fun guy, and along with Rodger you can't help but have a good time. With Joe thrown in the mix, look out! In addition to enjoying good company and good food, our sides were hurting from laughing so much.

After we returned to the boat, a local diver, who cleaned barnacles off the bottoms of boats at the marina, had noticed the name of our boat and wanted to know if it had anything to do with Indiana. Joe loves it when he is asked that question. The diver's girlfriend was from Indiana, and she would be thrilled to learn he had talked to some folks from there. He was a really interesting fellow who asked lots of questions about our boat.

Later Joe and I sat out in the cockpit enjoying the rest of the evening looking at the other boats across from us. It's interesting to read the names of the boats and try to figure out their meanings. People come up with some very interesting ones. We had a very good day with all our old and new friends.

We traveled 27.3 nautical miles today.

Sunday, April 27, 2003

We left the dock at 7:00 a.m. after a whirlwind Saturday getting everything done in one day (thanks to Denny). We made our way back out to the ICW, going under many bridges and passing shrimp boats bringing in their catch for the day. One shrimp boat seemed to have a dark cloud hanging over it, but in fact it was hundreds of sea gulls and dozens of pelicans flying around waiting for a handout. It's quite a sight to see and hear all these birds squawking at once. We could see and hear them a mile away.

We traveled through some luscious green marsh country. It's all we saw for miles and miles except for the porpoises playing all around us. Joe even saw two porpoises jump completely out of the water.

We anchored in the Bells River across from Fernandina Beach, Florida's northernmost city. It is located on Amelia Island east of the ICW. We are getting ready to cross over into Georgia waters.

We are also getting ready to cross sounds, which are large bodies of shallow water that can become very dangerous in just a short time if the wind should pick up from the wrong direction. Rodger and Dee have warned us about these sounds during our planning sessions. Joe has read about them and knows you have to wait for the right weather conditions to cross them. Since we put in a long day yesterday, we stopped early today.

It was a good day on the water. We traveled 57.8 nautical miles.

Monday, April 28, 2003

We pulled anchor at 7:00 a.m. this morning. Leaving the Bells River, we went into the Cumberland Sound and then into Georgia waters. The Kings Bay Submarine Base is located in this sound just north of the junction of St. Mary's River.

As we traveled across the sound, the coast guard pulled up on our starboard side in an R.I.B. inflatable and asked Joe to vacate the channel because a deep drafting vessel was coming through. Joe informed them that we were traveling with the boat ahead of us. The crewman said he would get them next and to go ahead and pull over. We both pulled our boats over out of the channel and waited to see what was coming through. An atomic submarine, half out of the water with some of the crew standing out on deck, was being guided by two large navy tugs, one pulling and one pushing. What a totally awesome sight! We couldn't believe that we got to watch this sub being brought into the base.

After getting back on our way in the Cumberland Sound, the weather started getting rough. Spray was coming over the bow and the waves made the boat pitch (rock forward and backward like a bucking horse) very badly. This is a situation when you are glad you have a pilothouse with inside steering.

Rodger radioed over and we decided to take an alternate route called the Umbrella Cut, which is a narrow shallow channel on the Cumberland River, thus avoiding St. Andrews Sound. It took us through Jekyll Sound and St. Simons Sound before we anchored in the Frederica River close to the remains of the Fort Frederica National Monument. There was not much left here—just a cannon and the American flag flying on one corner of the fort along the shoreline. You can take the dinghy over to the shore and go into town to find out about the history of the fort.

This was an excellent anchorage, so beautiful and serene. We were back off the channel with no one here but us. Rodger knew about this anchorage also.

Rodger and Dee rowed over to talk about our day and to see how we were doing so far. I'm glad Dee got some pictures of the submarine; I didn't even think to take any pictures. We were just in awe. I wonder where that submarine had been.

We traveled 46.5 nautical miles today.

Tuesday, April 29, 2003

We woke up to a bright sunny day perfect for boating. Rodger and Dee were ready to go when Joe radioed over to ask if it would be okay to stay here one more day because he needed a day to change the oil and filter. It was overdue and he's really religious about taking care of engine maintenance. Being the nice people they are, they said we could stay here one more day.

In such a situation, Dee just goes into her vacation mode. Joe worked on the boat, and I read a book and stayed out of the way. Joe takes up the whole boat whenever he works on the engine. After he had everything put together, I cleaned and straightened up the boat. Rodger and Dee went in the dinghy to check out the town and the memorial at the fort.

They came over to see if we wanted to go with them, but Joe had lots of work to do. He had finished installing the autopilot, but it didn't work. (Maybe someone needs to read the directions.) While we didn't make any miles, we had a beautiful day to relax and I got some boat cleaning done. This was a beautiful spot with a gentle breeze swaying through the trees all day.

You just have to stop and smell the sea breeze once in a while.

Wednesday, April 30, 2003

We pulled anchor at 7:00 a.m. It was a foggy morning so we took it a little slowly getting back out into the channel of the ICW, letting the sunshine burn off some of the fog.

The marshes were especially beautiful in the light morning mist, which creates an otherworldly landscape of grays and muted greens relieved only by egrets with their white feathers almost fluorescent against the green marsh grass. It was such a beautiful setting with the fog coming up off the water that I captured it on film by taking a picture of "Pockets" moving ahead of us.

With the fog lifted, we were back in the ICW traveling through miles of lush green marshland as far as the eye could see. It was absolutely breathtaking. On one of the islands we saw wild boar grazing.

We saw many shrimp boats trolling with their nets out, bringing in that delicious shrimp found out in the deep water. Rodger stood out on the stern of "Pockets" pointing west and shouting, "America is that way!" We laughed because we couldn't use our cell phones through here (no towers, no civilization).

I had hoped the wind would stay calm while we went through the Buttermilk, Sapello, and St. Catherine sounds. It ended up being a mild and pleasant day. Getting through all the sounds without any problems made this a really good day. We anchored in Big Tom Creek at 3:45 p.m.

We traveled 49.2 nautical miles today.

Thursday, May 1, 2003

We pulled anchor at 7:00 a.m. and headed back out to the ICW. We went up the Vernon River to the Savannah River, past a Sea Ray boat factory. Across the channel were many shrimp boats, their torn nets hanging from their outriggers and old ropes hanging from rusty hooks, abandoned after many years of service to their captains. These would have been the pride of the fleet back in their day!

Going through more marshland over to Calibougue Sound, which took us past Hilton Head, South Carolina, we saw an old abandoned lighthouse out on the point. It had warned captains about the shoreline surrounding it.

We went under more bridges, seeing restaurants and bait shops along the shore. We saw spectacular homes that looked like hotels; it's hard to believe that only one family lives in them.

I steered for a few miles today so that Joe could try to figure out why the autopilot is not working. Come to find out, someone (with initials J.P.) had wired it in backwards. Yahoo! It works now. Joe now feels better. The autopilot can steer the boat and give Joe a break from the wheel.

We had a good day on the water. We still haven't been able to use the cell phone; I guess civilization is still too far away. We anchored in Skull Creek just south of Port Royal Sound, South Carolina.

We traveled 50.8 nautical miles today.

Friday, May 2, 2003

We pulled anchor at 7:00 a.m. after having our coffee. We got ready to cross Port Royal Sound, which is five miles across, but found the water was getting rough. The tide was coming in and the wind was going out, which made for big wakes with white caps. We finally made it across the sound and up the river to Beaufort (pronounced "Bewfort"), South Carolina.

Today out in the ICW Joe saw the boat "Gypsy Rose," a 26-foot Nimble Kodiak, a sweet looking little sailboat. The captain writes interesting articles for a boating magazine Joe has read.

We pulled into the Downtown Marina in Beaufort at 9:45 a.m., ready for a hot shower and a good meal. The guys washed the salt off the boats while Dee and I did the laundry. After getting our chores done, everyone cleaned up and met at the marina office to go on foot to see the town.

While we were waiting for Rodger and Dee, the captain of the "Gypsy Rose" came by and Joe got to meet and talk with him. Captains are always ready to talk about their boats. Joe really enjoyed meeting him.

Rodger and Dee arrived ready to head to town to look for a place to eat. Beaufort is a beautiful small town with many historical buildings that can easily be seen on foot. Many of the houses are built in a style often used in the West Indies where the first floor is elevated over a high basement where the kitchen is located. A wide veranda often runs on three sides of the house. Many of the homes are set on bluffs overlooking the Beaufort River. It is an awesome view!

Joe wanted to find a hardware store to look for something for the boat. He always has some kind of an idea for the boat working in his head. Lots of good things can sometimes be found in hardware stores, so we don't mind stopping with him. Rodger remembered where one is located because they had stopped here once before. They wanted us to experience this town for ourselves, and I'm glad they did. We found the hardware store went in and looked around, but they didn't have what Joe was looking for.

Back out on the sidewalk, we walked a few blocks, passing many beautiful homes with flowers blooming abundantly. We stopped to look at lots of restaurant menus along the way and finally decided to eat at Ollie's. Joe loved it because it is the name of his good friend from work. We took a menu back with us to show Ollie. It was such a beautiful day that we sat at a table on the terrace. We ordered dinner, getting the salad bar. We had a coupon for a free bowl of she-crab soup, which we passed around for everyone to taste. It was certainly different. I let Joe have the rest of it because I'm not much of a seafood soup lover.

We were sitting, talking, and having a terrific time, as we always do, when a black bird flew in, landed on the table next to us and picked up a package of saltine crackers out of a basket. It opened the crackers with its beak and feet and ate them. He had obviously done this before, and we found it entertaining. After just a few weeks on the water, we don't need much to entertain us.

After enjoying our delicious meal, we walked back through town. The guys decided we needed some ice cream to top off the evening. They just happened to remember that we had earlier walked past an ice cream store. We enjoyed a delicious chocolate malt there. Continuing through town, we worked our way back to the marina for the night.

I'm so glad we stopped in this charming town. We had a short day on the water so there was time to see the town of Beaufort. We had a wonderful day together on land!

We traveled 15.3 nautical miles today.

Saturday, May 3, 2003

Leaving the dock at 6:45 a.m., we dropped in behind "Pockets." We headed to Charleston, South Carolina, today. Rodger and Dee can have a short visit with their daughter, Lauren, who lives close by. The wind had picked up a little, and we discussed pulling into Ross Marina instead of trying to make it into Charleston. When Rodger tried to pull into a slip at the marina, the wind was so strong that it actually blew him into another boat (no damage done, thank goodness). He had no control over the vessel because of the wind. They radioed to tell us not to try pulling in; it was impossible to get up to the docks. We just went on into Charleston, arriving at 5:45 p.m.

We had called ahead for reservations at the City Marina, but since we arrived a day early we were not sure they would be able to get us in. Fortunately, they had slips available (we lucked out again). This is the most beautiful marina we have been in so far. It has emerald green tile in the shower rooms and a courtesy van that takes you to town and picks you up. We could finally use our cell phone, and, wouldn't you know it, Dee's quit working. She borrowed mine to call Lauren to let her know we were here a day early and also to call a cell phone store in town.

After taking a refreshing shower, we ate dinner on board and just relaxed on the boat this evening after fighting the wind all day.

Joe changed over to statute miles because of the intercoastal mile markers are marked that way. We traveled 66 miles today, and a total of 661.2 statute miles for the whole trip so far.

Sunday, May 4, 2003

Lauren arrived this morning. She is just a bright beam of sunshine, cute as a kitten, and nice on top of all that. We girls headed to the phone store to see what was wrong with Dee's phone. The transformer had gone out, but they no longer had parts for her phone (one year old). Dee had computer equipment on the boat for this phone to hook into, but all we got was "sorry, you have to buy a new phone." While we were standing in line to see about a new phone, the technician called Dee back over to tell her he had the transformer that she needed. It had been taken from a phone traded in by a customer who had upgraded his phone. The technician fixed Dee's phone free of charge and sent us on our way. What a deal! Dee had good luck today.

We made a quick stop at the grocery to pick up some staples before heading back to the marina to meet the guys. They had taken the courtesy van from the marina to a West Marine store in town. Joe had to order a blue chip (a water chart) for the GPS (Global Positioning System), which he would pick up at our next stop up the waterway.

We were anxious to see this beautiful old historic town of Charleston, South Carolina, which is located on a small peninsula between the Cooper and Ashley rivers. The Cooper is the industrial river, and all the pleasure-boat facilities are located on the Ashley. This is another great stopover. You can walk or bicycle to the downtown stores, which are about a mile from the marina. Many of the old houses are within walking distance, or you can take the bus.

I can see why they filmed movies here. There are flowers blooming everywhere you look, fragrant flowering vines on fences, and perfectly landscaped yards. Even the alleys were decorated with pots of flowers of all colors and with containers of greenery in all shapes and sizes. The air is perfumed from the blossoming flowers and trees. This town is picture perfect. We walked along the waterfront past a huge pineapple water fountain, taking pictures of each other in front of it. The wind was really blowing (not a good hair day), but we still walked from one end to the other.

Over at the Battery you can look out across Ashley River to the island where Fort Sumter is located and where the first shots of the Civil War were fired. Big navy ships were docked here displaying their colors, making you proud to be an American!

We walked down Rainbow Row where the houses are all quite colorful and are built one on top of another. Antique brass doorknobs adorn their big wooden doors, and tall wrought iron fences and gates are covered with the heavenly smell of flowering honeysuckle vines. Many of the houses are built with the front facing the side yard. Most have two stories with balconies decorated with potted flowers. Chairs on balconies encourage sitting out to enjoy the warm afternoon breezes. Cobblestone streets with their old mansions caused us to feel we were stepping back in time.

There was not enough time in one day to take in all of Charleston, so we called for the courtesy van to pick us up. Our friend Charlie Hall from Oyster Bay Marina back in St. Augustine had told us about a restaurant here where we had to have dinner. He had given us directions to the place, but he must have left out a turn or two. We stopped to ask a local for help and finally found it off the beaten path. The Richards and Charlene, named for the shipwreck back in the 1800's, was unique, to say the least. Walking through the door and down a hallway, we saw large old pictures of the famous wreck on display, along with old newspaper articles that told its story.

The waitress took us past the kitchen into a dimly lit room with rough-sawed wooden round tables covered with white meat-wrapping paper. Lanterns sat in the center of the tables, so it was like a candlelight dinner. Then the waitress handed all of us a menu printed on a sheet of plain white paper with a colored marker to circle our dinner choices.

We all ordered a shrimp dinner that included red rice, homemade slaw, hush puppies, and excellent sweet iced tea. Joe had shrimp, scallops, oysters, and flounder. I had grilled shrimp with red rice, homemade slaw, hush puppies, and sweet tea.

Everything was so DELICIOUS! I'm glad they didn't charge for atmosphere; we couldn't have afforded it.

Everything was disposable; so, when we left, all that the waitress had to do was pull up the corners of the white paper and the table was clean and ready for the next customer. Good idea! Thanks, Charlie that was a great place and an excellent dinner!

We headed back to the marina, stuffed full after having a wonderful dinner with great company and conversation. We were thankful Lauren came to visit with a car and was willing to go on a wild goose chase to find this place back off the main roads. It truly was a once-in-a-lifetime dining experience and fun night.

Monday, May 5, 2003

This morning we met Rodger, Dee, and Lauren on the dock in front of the boats and walked over to a local restaurant for breakfast before taking the courtesy van back into town.

Today we went to the Market Place in downtown Charleston. The market is in a section of town where there is everything you can imagine—restaurants, craft shops, flea market, candy shops, clothing shops galore, and lots of silver jewelry shops. (Right, Rodger?)

I caught Joe standing in front of the "Gone with the Wind" Rhett Butler store with a "Frankly, my dear, I don't give a damn" T-shirt hanging in the window right behind him. I had to take his picture because I think Joe could be the next Rhett, you know!! (But I haven't convinced Joe yet.) I bought a T-shirt with cats dressed up like Rhett and Scarlett.

Dee found lots of goodies for her granddaughter Sydney. They call her Ladybug, and Dee found many cute things for her with ladybugs on them. After going through the shops, we went sightseeing to look at more fabulous homes. Joe wanted to find a hardware store (go figure). He is still looking for that item for the boat.

On the way we came across a New York hot dog vendor along the sidewalk, and Dee and I had to have one just for a snack. I gave my last bite to Joe so we could say we had a New York Dog. It was delicious!!

We finally found an ACE hardware and went inside. I couldn't believe my eyes; there were real cats in the store making themselves at home on the store shelves. Now this is my kind of hardware store. But they still didn't have what Joe was looking for. (No surprise.)

When we had just about walked off the soles of our shoes, we headed back to the main street to call for the courtesy van to pick us up.

Here's Joe standing in front of store.

Back at the marina, Joe had a Taco Bell attack. We checked with Rodger and Dee to see what they were doing for dinner. They had never had a taco chicken salad. Lauren said, "I'll drive. It is one of my favorite places to eat, also." To which Joe replied, "Good, you drive and I will buy your dinner." We all climbed into her vehicle and went looking for a Taco Bell restaurant. This proved to be another wild goose chase!

Going down the highway, we saw a group of kids up ahead on the side of the road running out to cars and handing something to them.

We found they were giving out free slices of Papa John's pizza. These boys took one look at Lauren and gave her the whole box of pizza (being a cutie really helps). When we got to the next stop sign where there were more kids, girls this time, we were given another whole pizza free. I think they were ready to go home. Another lucky day!

We each had a whole pizza for our next day's meal on the boat (good deal—no cooking!). We finally found Taco Bell and went in. With all that free pizza, there we were eating taco salad, laughing about the whole experience. We had such a good time; it seems we have been friends forever.

Back at the marina we got everything ready to take off early the next morning. We hated having to say goodbye to Lauren. She was such a good sport to drive us around and put up with us crazy old folks. Thanks, Lauren!

Tuesday, May 6, 2003

We were up early to say goodbye to Lauren with hugs and a kiss. She is a really sweet young lady. We settled our bill at the office and got ready to head out. It has been a really fun three days. Charleston is a beautiful historical place to visit.

At 6:45 a.m. we were pulling away from the docks, heading into the channel and traveling through more marshland to Winyah Bay past Georgetown, South Carolina.

It was a long day going upstream with a 20 mph wind, which caused really rough steering. We anchored outside Georgetown in Sampit Point. We were ready to drop anchor tonight after fighting the wind all day. It has been a lot more physical than Joe imagined, and it takes all your energy to keep on course while holding the wheel for hours at a time if there is a very strong current or wind. I helped some, and I can see that having another person at the helm is a big help. You are ready to drop anchor at the end of a good day and relax. Joe will certainly sleep well tonight.

We traveled 66 miles.

Wednesday, May 7, 2003

We pulled anchor at 9:00 a.m. after sleeping in this morning. We went through miles and miles of narrow marshland as we headed for the Waccamaw River. The Waccamaw is a beautiful section of the waterway, which many consider to be the loveliest part. It is A Young Man's Dream / An Old Man's Reality

very beautiful through here with areas of swamps, marshes, endless creeks, and dense forests. Along the banks is abandoned rice fields with unused canals overhung by live oaks with long strands of Spanish moss draped over many of their branches. We saw eagles perched on dead tree branches looking for a bite to eat. The eagle is one of the most awesome birds in the wild.

There we saw cormorants, gulls, and ducks lined up on pilings at deserted docks along the waterway drying out their feathers. We even saw some wood storks flying over; they seem too big to be flying.

We took the lead today and picked the anchorage, a beautiful spot back in Enterprise Creek. The anchorage is in a little cove that is peaceful and quiet. We have seen many kinds of birds, including woodpeckers; Joe thought he heard turkeys. We have found so many nice places like this, and I love it when we find a good anchorage. It is just "Whoosher" and "Pockets" and Mother Nature at her best!

This evening we had Rodger and Dee over for snacks and discussing tomorrow's journey. It is nice to have someone traveling with you both to discuss and plan things and to have companionship. It also makes you feel safer having another boat traveling with you. Rodger usually has about three days planned ahead. That is good! You need a plan B in case plan A doesn't work.

We traveled 31 miles today.

Thursday, May 8, 2003

Pulling anchor at 7:30 a.m., we left our peaceful anchorage, headed back into the ICW, and went through some very pretty countryside. Cypress knees stuck up through the water all along the shore. A six-foot log lying in the water held turtles sunning themselves all the way across it.

We headed for Barefoot Landing where you can dock for the night free (no electric or water), but we are staying overnight just to go through the factory outlet stores. (Oh boy, shopping!) The dock was not very long so we rafted (tied together side by side) to "Pockets" so more boats could dock here. This means that we have to walk across "Pockets" to get to the dock.

Going ashore, the guys headed for (you guessed it) the hardware store, and Dee and I went to the Barefoot General Store, which resembles an old time five-and-dime back in the good old days. We had a hot dog and sat out in the rocking chairs on the front porch, just relaxing. The guys found us, and we went arm in arm looking in the various shops. It was good to walk and stretch our legs.

We found a Damon's Restaurant where we thought we would have dinner. We were ready for a good meal! Being good, we had B.B.Q. chicken, but afterwards we found a fudge-and-nut shop. I bought some chocolate covered peanut brittle. YUMMY! So much for being good!

Joe took a handful of nuts they were giving as samples and also a sample of a green pea covered with Australian horseradish. He said that one of those was enough; it was HOT!

There were snow leopards and a Siberian tiger on display here. They are gorgeous animals, but I hate to see them in cages.

Joe found a good deal on a pair of deck shoes. Rodger also looked for a pair but could not find any like Joe's in his size. Joe wore his out of the store, and we continued walking around some more.

On the walkway we found a stand that sold a different type of souvenir. Your name is written on one side of a tiny grain of rice, and another name of your choice is written on the other side. The grain of rice is then put in a small tube of colored water; the tube is placed on a key chain as a souvenir. I couldn't resist this because I never find my name on anything. Now I have a souvenir of our fun time here.

Joe and I had a picture taken with our heads stuck through a big board, making it appear we were wearing hula skirts. I'm sure you can picture this in your head. We have had a good time at this stop. If we had been by ourselves, we might not have stopped here—so, thanks, Rodger and Dee.

Joe and I at Barefoot Landing having Fun
"TIKI JIM"S"

We were docked outside Gregg Norman's restaurant, The Australian Grill. They had live entertainment with a band and singer. This was nice for the boaters docked here. We sat out in the cockpit of the boat, relaxing, listening to the music, and talking about the fun we had shared today. We are so glad Rodger and Dee wanted to stop here at Barefoot Landing. Another great day was had by all!

We traveled 22.7 miles today.

Friday, May 9, 2003

Up early, we untied the boats from each other and pushed off, carefully getting back out in the ICW heading for the Little River. To get there we had to go through Pine Island Cut. This land cut is an extremely narrow three-mile-long section called the Rock Pile, with rocky ledges on both sides of the channel. Although the rocks create a picturesque scene, it is a hazardous section. Pleasure boats must be aware of oncoming traffic because there is not enough room to pass safely if you meet a barge. Therefore, you must call ahead on the radio to see if anyone is coming from the opposite direction before going around bends in the channel.

The banks along the cut are constantly being eroded by the wash from vessels. The soil is being washed away from the roots of trees on the bank's edge so badly that the trees have nothing to hold them up, causing them to fall into the canal. You have to watch for falling trees and also for roots that can be a danger to your boat's hull and prop, especially if they are partially or completely under water and can't be seen. One of my jobs was to watch for debris so we didn't hit anything. Can you picture me perched out on the bow like a hood ornament looking for debris in the water?

The banks, as well as the trees, are covered with wild honeysuckle vines that fill the air with their wonderful aroma. There's driftwood all along the shore, making a good place for wildlife to land on or hide under. I would have liked to take some of the driftwood back home.

Getting to the Little River, we had to wait for the pontoon bridge at Sunset Beach, North Carolina, to open. This bridge is on floating pontoons, and we had to call ahead to request passage through. A cable cranked by hand moved the pontoon around to open the waterway so we could get through. Then it was closed so motorists could get back across the bridge. This was an interesting procedure to watch.

On down the river we saw dozens of goats out on a spoil. A spoil is a pile of sand dredged by the Army Corps of Engineers that makes an island out in the waterway. We wondered how the goats got out there and what they ate because we didn't see any vegetation around.

We passed many inlets that would take you out into the Atlantic Ocean where the water is a beautiful Caribbean azure blue with miles and miles of white sandy beaches. People were out collecting shells in buckets, digging for clams, and enjoying the warm sunny day. There were porpoises playing alongside the boat. What a sight to see!

We anchored at the Masonboro Boat Yard and Marina located in Wilmington, North Carolina. This is a large live-aboard marina, which means people can live here on their boats. Custom yachts are built here and the yard has a reputation for fine craftsmanship. A courtesy van is also available upon request. We checked in at the office to get our slips and asked to use the courtesy van tomorrow. A slip is a space at a dock where your boat is tied up for the night.

After a shower, we met on the big porch for food and drink and had a wonderful time talking about old times. We found out that Rodger and Joe are so much alike it is scary. Besides being Hoosiers, they think alike and have such a good time talking to each other.

Dee and I enjoy sharing stories about our families. It's still hard to believe we have known these two for only a few months. We enjoy talking and laughing with each other. I guess, when you think about it, it's really a small world out there.

The folks at this marina have been very nice, friendly, and helpful. So far, we haven't met any bad people traveling on the waterways.

We had another very enjoyable day and relaxing evening with our friends.

We traveled 66 miles today.

Saturday, May 10, 2003

We were up at 8:00 a.m. and walked over to the office to get the keys to the marina courtesy van. We met Kevin, the young man who runs the yard during the weekend; he has an Elvis look about him. We headed to the West Marine store in town to get the blue chip Joe had ordered back in Charleston.

We thought the store didn't open till 9:00; therefore, we had time to stop at McDonald's for breakfast. We discovered, though, that the store opened at 8:00, but stopping for breakfast is always nice. The GPS blue-chip chart was waiting for Joe at West Marine.

While returning to the marina, we discovered the van wasn't running on all cylinders and were not sure we would make it back. There was no back seat in the van. Dee and I improvised by putting paper towels on the greasy, filthy floor. We knelt on the towels; we were glad we didn't have far to go in this position. Still, we made a fun trip out of having to sit on our knees!

After returning to the marina, we untied at 10:00 a.m., heading back out to the ICW. On Saturdays boat traffic is usually heavy (the guys call them weekend warriors), and today it was heavy. This made for a stressful day because we had to weave our way through all the boaters out water skiing or tubing.

Going through some shoal water, we grounded (bumped bottom), but that little extra horsepower in our engine comes in handy at times like this. It certainly gave us a scare for a few minutes.

We went past a point of land on our port side (left) where a house, painted bright pink, had a huge lighthouse in the front yard, also painted pink. Not very many pink lighthouses are seen on the waterway. Some homes have a cupola on the roof that gives the homeowner a place to look out on the water. It is a good idea to have a lookout on top of a house on the waterway. There would certainly be much to see both up and down the river.

Going past an old abandoned lighthouse in Morehead City, North Carolina, I thought about the history of these old lighthouses and the stories they could tell. They meant so much to sailors long ago, as well as today.

At 3:40 we anchored for the night at Mile Hammock Bay. The entrance through here is very shallow, so we had to go slowly. In case the wind should pick up during the night, we stayed in deep water and made sure our anchor was set. This is part of a military base back here. We could see military personnel on shore doing maneuvers. We saw them get into their boats and leave without making a sound. We hope they don't do any shooting overnight.

We traveled 43.4 miles.

Sunday, May 11, 2003

We pulled anchor at 6:45 a.m. and started up the ICW, going past Camp Lejeune. There is a four-mile-long military firing range here. If it is occupied, you have to get permission to go past it, especially if there is firing practice. We lucked out as it was quiet today, and we went right on past without any problems.

We passed under more bridges and through some really shallow water where the birds looked like they were walking on water. They actually were on a spoil of sand and seashells, just barely covered with water. This made us do a double take.

We approached a bridge that "Pockets" couldn't get under. They need a 17-foot clearance and had to radio ahead to the bridge tender to raise it for them. We need only a 12-foot clearance without our mast so we can get under most of the bridges. This in one of the reasons we left the mast back in Fort Myers. Sometimes you have to wait a while for the bridge to be raised, and that really slows you down. Plus, having to idle back and forth in the water while waiting burns up fuel and often taxes our patience.

We went through Bogue Sound. Through here there's just a small strip of land called a barrier island between the ICW and the Atlantic Ocean. We could see out over the barrier island, and it looked like you could just drop right off the earth. The water blends right into the sky, making it look like it goes on forever. The view was truly awesome. If you didn't know the earth is round, it could really be a scary feeling looking out over the horizon from a boat. This made me think how frightening it must have been for the sailors years ago because is looks scary to me right now!

After getting through the sound, we went through Morehead City, South Carolina, and then up the Newport River. We stopped at Sea Gate Marina located just off the river. It was windy today, making the water rough. We were glad to get into port and docked for the night and to be able to turn off the engine and relax. It's stressful, but there's something about it that makes you want to go on. You want to know what's ahead on the river or around the next bend that you haven't seen yet.

After getting into the marina, checked in and secured in our slip, we noticed there was one lonely Canada goose with a broken wing out in the yard. It was trying to make friends with the ducks that were hanging out. There were several ducks and it looked as though they were all going to be friends.

Dee and I walked up to the office to check out our surroundings. We found a nice TV/sitting room where books could be exchanged if you wish to share yours after reading them. Boaters read a lot and this is a good way to exchange books. Most of the marinas have book exchanges.

The weather was not looking good, and it looked like we might be here at least two more days. This would give an opportunity to meet more people. We have met some really nice people while staying in the marinas thus far.

Walking down the docks to visit "Pockets," we noticed a man sitting out in the cockpit of his boat playing a guitar. Joe also plays, so, being interested, we stopped and introduced ourselves. Rodger and Dee came down also and we met his wife, Denise. She mentioned they had a car and she was going to a Super Wal-Mart tomorrow. When asked if Dee and I would like to go, we answered in unison that we would if she didn't mind us going along. So, it looks like we are going shopping tomorrow.

It will be nice to get off the boat and walk around without the back-and-forth rocking motion under you.

We went back to the boat, had a good dinner and a pleasant evening.

We traveled 51.7 miles today.

Monday, May 12, 2003

Denise came over this morning to tell us she would be going to town about noon. Dee and I were ready and met her on the dock, excited to be going on a girls'-day-out shopping trip. Denise told us to take our time shopping because she was not in a hurry.

Dee and I enjoyed our shopping spree and stocked up on a lot of things you can find only at Wally World. We almost couldn't get it all in her car. We gave Denise a bouquet of flowers to show our appreciation; she was a super nice lady. She took us to another store for wine, then on a little tour around town to show us some of the places of interest. We drove along the waterfront to look at the boat docks there. I think Denise was as ready as Dee and I were for a girls' day out. We had a wonderful afternoon making a new friend. Again, we were fortunate to find a boater with a vehicle. She knew that those living on boats always need supplies because of the limited space to store things.

Getting back with our goodies, we loaded them in one of the little carts all marinas conveniently provide. We looked up the dock to see the guys coming to help.

31

The folks operating this marina were nice, friendly, down home people. They were going to have a cookout one evening for those at the marina. The only bad thing here is that they have Pluto water (smells like rotten eggs) and we couldn't fill the boat's water tanks.

The little swallows that perched on the lifelines of the boat made such a mess while singing to us that we tried to discourage them from staying very long.

Since we will be here for a few days because of foul weather, Joe took advantage of the time by working on the boat and changing the oil and filters.

We went to visit Rodger and Dee this evening to discuss what we would be doing the next few days. They are getting us ready to be on our own. It's been really easy following them; they have helped us learn where to anchor and which marinas to pull into. I have helped Joe with the channel markers, with docking at the marinas, with the ropes, with pushing off when we leave so we don't scrape the sides of the boat, and with getting off safely. I can see how much easier it is to have two people, but one could do it if necessary.

It has been fun traveling with Rodger and Dee; we have seen so many interesting sights. I've taken some really good pictures, and Joe wouldn't be able to take any if he were by himself. I started thinking about what I will miss by not going on—including Joe—if I get off with "Pockets" in Virginia. It has been an interesting trip so far and I'm glad I did this. Dee keeps asking me if I've made up my mind yet; she is worried about Joe going on by himself.

Honestly, I don't think anyone else would put up with Joe's moods. They would have thrown him overboard by now. This is more challenging and tiring after a day fighting the wheel and the waves than Joe thought it would be. The autopilot is not much help in rough water and in going through the narrow canals. I hope it works when we get in more open waters like the Great Lakes so he can get a break from the wheel once in a while.

Tuesday, May 13, 2003

The wind has been blowing 15-20 miles per hour now for two days, so we are still at the Sea Gate Marina. We walked down to "Pockets" and visited with Rodger and Dee again this afternoon to go over the next few days of travel. You start getting stir crazy just sitting around and not moving; just getting off the boat helps and I'm sure they feel the same way. Rodger likes to go over the agenda with Joe. He has been giving Joe a few pointers on how far to try to go each day and not to try pushing it until getting very tired. He advised Joe to get into port before dark if at all possible and just to be smart with his actions and decisions. I know Joe knows all this, but having Rodger tell him is important. He has done this a few times and knows how badly you sometimes want to go just a little farther, but it's not worth it. Joe respects Rodger's knowledge of the water and will take his advice seriously. They enjoy just sitting and talking to each other.

Dee asked if I'm going to continue the trip. She knows that an extra set of hands is valuable. She helps Rodger a lot, even does a lot of the steering. Joe's ankles have been swelling from sitting at the wheel so long, and I have been steering some so he can put them up a while to ease the swelling. I can see it helps to have an extra hand. The Erie Canal with all the locks will be a big challenge. I don't see anyone else doing this and still be friends at the end. Under stress Joe can be a bear. So far, it has been fun for the most part. Sometimes there can be too much togetherness, but love prevails.

Calm winds are predicted for tomorrow, and we want to be ready to go. It's good that Rodger, The Planner, has everything mapped out. We are going to miss them when they leave us to go home. I don't like to think about it. I'm probably going to be the planner if I go on. Since this was Joe's dream, I want him to do as much as possible so he gets this boating dream out of his system for a while. (Don't tell Joe this.)

I fixed dinner on board and we relaxed on the boat tonight. It is much easier to fix dinner while tied to a dock and hooked up to electric with hot water to clean up. We are getting everything put up and ready just in case we get to leave early tomorrow.

We hope tomorrow is a good day for boating.

Wednesday, May 14, 2003

This morning the wind had calmed down and we were ready to get back to the Great Circle trip. We untied the boat from the dock at the marina this morning at 6:45 a.m. and got back out into the channel.

Following "Pockets" through Adams Creek, we found this narrow passage to be slow going over to the Big Neuse River. The Neuse River is another body of water that can be as bad as, or even worse than, Albemarle Sound in a blow. This river, like the sound, is shallow and prone to the same kind of steep uncomfortable seas. You must wait for the right weather window again before venturing into it; listening to the weather on the marine radio is essential.

The weather looked good for crossing the river, and it looked like we would not have any problems. We went through Bay River and Goose Creek. All of these creeks are really shallow, narrow, and slow going. We crossed the Pamlico River, another big body of water. I never really thought about how much of the earth is covered with water, but I've been told about three fourths of the earth is covered. They have me convinced; there is a lot of water out here. Goes to show you how much I know!

Someone is watching over us from above; we got through these big waters today without any problems. Thank you, Lord!

We headed up Pungo River to Dowry Creek Marina. Dee called ahead to make reservations. The marine radio weather channel was again predicting 10 to 25 mph winds for the next few days. You certainly want to be back in a marina tied to a dock in those conditions. The weather is so unpredictable you must always be prepared for delays. Plan ahead and listen to the weather channel.

Dowry Creek Marina is located near Belhaven, North Carolina. This is another beautiful marina with its white office building up on pilings and water flowers along the water's edge. You walk over a bridge with more water lilies and flowering water plants to the shower and lounge. The TV room and book exchange library are located in a building that is also on pilings. A big front porch with rocking chairs makes it seem just like home. With a picture postcard view, this is a nice stopover for any boater.

The couple living here owns the marina, and their welcome makes you feel like family. After getting the boat tied in the slip at the dock, we headed for the showers. You really appreciate these showers when you don't have one on your boat. Our next boat will have a shower on board, according to the captain.

We met Rodger and Dee on the porch with our drinks and snacks and enjoyed the wonderful breeze and beautiful surroundings here. Dee and I took the rocking chairs, just enjoying each other's company. I really have enjoyed having her to talk to; she has been a godsend for me. Besides becoming good friends, we have a good time talking, laughing, and sharing with each other about our lives and children and grandchildren. We have missed our kids.

Rodger and Joe have been in their own world talking about when they were young boys back in Indiana and inventing things they have dreamed up in their heads. They finish each other's sentences; Dee and I have decided they are out of the same pea pod. They have certainly enjoyed boating together and have formed a bond that most brothers would love to share.

One of the two resident cats at the marina likes cheese crackers. We shared ours with them.

We went back to our boats for dinner. We listened to the weather channel because weather conditions were not looking good. This could mean staying here an extra day unless it changes. Weather certainly controls our days on the water.

We traveled 62 miles today.

Thursday, May 15, 2003

After having breakfast and coffee, the guys went to the marina office to watch the TV weather channel and to check the radar to see what's going on. They came back shouting, "Good news, let's go!" The wind would be 5 to 10 mph today. This is the weather window I referred to. Good weather must be taken advantage of because it can change quickly and leave you stranded.

At 9:30 a.m. we pulled away from the docks waving goodbye to the owner, Ted, who was having a beer-chicken cookout today for everyone here at the marina. So far, our luck has not been very good for attending the marina BBQ's.

On the way out we stopped to get the holding tank pumped out. We went up the Pungo River to the ICW, heading for the Alligator River. The Pungo and Alligator River canals are both densely wooded. There are swamps and patches of marsh grass on both sides. This made me wonder what critters are down in these waters.

There are cattle ranches on both sides of the canal. Cattle stood in the water staring at us as we passed by, wondering what we were doing in their drinking water. We had to stay in the middle of the channel through this cut; keep a lookout for submerged stumps, debris, and bank erosion; and watch the depth gauge closely. Both boats need at least four feet to float. Despite the name, we found no alligators in the Alligator River. We pulled into the Alligator Marina for the night.

Rodger needed fuel, and this is both a truck stop and a marina. We found a good price on diesel. There is a very nice shower house here, and we enjoyed another wonderful hot shower.

We walked over to the restaurant at the truck stop for a BBQ sandwich. We all got the special: BBQ sandwich with fries and slaw. We took our food back to "Pockets" and ate together.

This North Carolina BBQ is made with a vinegar base, not tomato. The sandwich did not sit well on my stomach, making me wish I hadn't eaten it. I hope I feel better tomorrow; it's not fun being sick at your stomach on a moving boat.

We traveled 48 miles today.

Friday, May 16, 2003

We were up early this morning, and after breakfast and coffee we pulled away from the dock at 6:20 a.m., leaving Alligator Marina. With very little wind, we left the ICW and took a short cut across Albemarle Sound.

I helped Joe watch for crab pots. A small Styrofoam ball identifies the location of a pot; the ball is attached to a rope that is tied to the pot, which is baited to catch crabs. The pots can be placed anywhere, but are usually placed along the edge of a channel. They are covered with algae and are very difficult to see in the blue-green water until you are on top of one. It is not good to get a propeller tangled in one.

The sky did not look good, but we crossed the sound without any problems once again. We went past a tug pushing thousands of pounds of wood chips up the Pasquotank River. The river where it leaves the sound is narrow for about four miles, but it takes you through some wonderful wildlife country.

We are headed to Elizabeth City, North Carolina, where we can stay free at the courtesy dock for 48 hours. We needed to get there early because it fills up fast, especially if the weather is bad. It is just a few blocks from town, which is convenient.

At noon we were heading in. The river was becoming choppy, and getting through the harbor was rough. The wind was blowing us around, listing the boat over. It felt like we were going to tip all the way over; I didn't like it even though I knew it wouldn't go over.

The wind was cold, and it was a rainy, very nasty day. The city dock here is called The Mariner's Wharf. Fighting the wind and rain, we tied the boat to the pilings. The weather finally cleared enough for us to get out to stretch our legs.

Dee and I were checking out the pier when a gentleman in a golf cart pulled up, welcomed us to the city, and introduced himself as Fred Fearing. He told us he was 84 years young. You could tell that he loved his work. He told us he had known the Wright brothers, and he had other interesting stories about the town to tell us. He invited us to a wine and cheese party at the wharf this afternoon, weather permitting. Asking us to sign his register, he then handed us some clippers and told us we could cut a rose from the rose garden in front of the welcome building. What a nice welcome!

Dee and I each cut a rose and headed back to put them in a vase and to tell the guys about being invited to a wine and cheese party later in the afternoon here at the docks. This was a first for us at a city dock, and what a nice surprise!

It was still misting rain and my stomach was still not good. Joe didn't think I needed to go to the party under the circumstances, so we walked to town to look around and get a good meal in my tummy. Getting into town, we found a hardware store. As it turned out, I was glad we stopped there.

I found a baking pan I had been looking for that makes individual angel food cakes. The hardware owner had a miniature schnauzer dog in the store and it followed us everywhere. They are cute little dogs.

Walking a few more blocks, we found an inviting hometown diner called The Colonial Restaurant. We had delicious steak dinners; I was soon feeling better, thank goodness.

We headed back toward the wharf and stopped at a craft consignment shop. Everything in the shop—jewelry, paintings, painted glass items, pottery, woodcarvings, etc.—was handmade by local people. I loved this store; craft stores are my weakness. I got some good ideas there that I want to try. I could have spent hours there.

Farther down the block we stopped at a clothing consignment shop. I needed a pair of warm pants. Then we headed over to the town's main highway where we found an Ace hardware store and a CVS that could refill our prescriptions. Walking back to the boat, we passed a shrimp restaurant that looked like a good place to eat with Rodger and Dee.

Elizabeth City is another city full of history. The Wright brothers made their first flight from here. A blimp factory can be seen from the harbor. A blimp in front of the factory looked like a giant unpainted egg. Tours through the factory are available.

Walking through town we saw beautiful magnolia trees in full bloom in the yards of many old homes. They don't build homes like they used to; I love these magnificent old houses in these towns. We also learned they grow potatoes here and have an Albemarle Potato Festival every year with a Little Miss Spud contest and a potato recipe contest. This would be an interesting event to attend.

The weather was still cold and rainy. I hadn't brought anything warm to wear, so I'm glad we found that clothing store. I couldn't believe how cold it was.

Getting back to the boat, we found Rodger and Dee waiting. They worried about us when we didn't show up at the party and when we didn't answer their knock at our boat. We should have told them we were going for a walk so they wouldn't worry about us. We explained everything to them, and they were happy I was feeling better. I was glad I was feeling better, too!

We traveled 33.8 miles today.

Saturday, May 17, 2003

We were up having breakfast only to discover the weather was still cold and rainy. We noticed another sailboat coming into the city dock, so the guys went out to help. It's always nice to get a helping hand while coming into a dock, but especially so on a nasty day when the wind is

39

so strong. It was an older couple traveling with their grandson on a 32-foot Bayfield sailboat named "Rainbow Connection" from Canada. The captain, Don, who is a 72-year-young man, had a 15-year-old grandson named Jamel. I told Jamel that his name was beautiful, and he told us that's what it means in Arabic. He was a handsome looking young man, so adorable and helpful. We all fell in love with him. He didn't just walk around the boat; he jumped and climbed around like a monkey. We all enjoyed watching him; it was a pleasure having him around.

On board they had a Jack Russell terrier named Fluffy, which wore a little yellow doggy lifejacket. We thought the name was humorous because those dogs are not fluffy. She loved Jamel and barked up a storm whenever he was out of her sight. I can't imagine traveling with a dog on board.

It finally stopped raining so we could get off the boat to walk around. We noticed that many of the local people come here to the wharf to eat their lunch or to sit on a bench to look out at the water and the boats. We felt like we were on display.

We told Rodger and Dee about the shrimp restaurant we found yesterday; they thought this sounded like a good place to eat. After dinner, we walked back to the hardware store. We decided we should stop at the DQ for ice cream before walking back to the boats. We got back to the boats just in time because rain started falling again.

While going back, we walked past Antioch Church. With its faded pink paint, it became a photo opportunity, and I hurried back with my camera to take its picture before the rain got too bad. I wish I could find out about its history. Joe was standing out on the boat looking for me to return. (Oops!)

Tomorrow has to be a better day.

Sunday, May 18, 2003

We pulled away from the docks at Elizabeth City at 6:45 a.m., and "Rainbow Connection" decided to come along with us for company.

We think Jamel likes having all of us to talk to and hang out with. We all enjoy having him around and are glad they are joining us. It's good to travel in a group in case there is a problem.

We needed to meet a 7:00 a.m. bridge opening at the Elizabeth City bascule bridge. It opens each hour on the hour; we didn't want to wait till 8:00.

Turner's Cut, a three-and-one-half-mile land cut to the entrance of the beautiful Pasquotank River, is not much wider than the canal itself. It winds and twists around for miles and then goes through the South Mills Lock, where we were raised up nine feet. We had a pleasant passage through here.

All boats must moor to the west wall, so the fenders must be out on the port (left) side. A fender is a hard plastic device on a rope hung over the side of the boat to protect the sides from any damage caused by rubbing against the cement walls of the locks. As we went through the locks, I stood on the bow (front) of the boat and held the rope to keep us from drifting away from the wall when the water starts to raise or lower the boat in the lock. It was raining just enough for me to be soaked. (I didn't have any rain gear.) Joe was in the cockpit under the bimini staying dry. (What's wrong with this picture?)

After getting through these locks, we went inside to steer, and I put on dry clothes. Joe said I should get some rain gear as soon as we find a store that sells it. It was a gloomy day out on the water.

We stopped at the North Carolina Visitors Center located on the canal and State Road 17. We thought the center would be open and we could get maps and information about the state. However, it was closed, so Jamel, Dee, and I walked over to a grocery for some fresh bread and milk, Coke, and fresh fruit. Jamel carried the groceries back across the highway for us.

The water is very good here, so we filled our water bottles and the water tanks on the boats. By staying here overnight, we can start up the

Dismal Swamp early tomorrow. It's still misting rain with a chill in the air. I wish it would get warm!\

We traveled 23.7 miles today.

Monday, May 19, 2003

We were up early, ready to head north on the Dismal Swamp Canal, a 26.4-mile land cut with a controlling depth of 6 feet. Because shallower depths can be encountered, the speed limit is only 7 mph. Since that's our speed anyway, that won't be a problem for us.

The Dismal Swamp is not dismal at all, and it doesn't even look like a swamp. Its name came from what local folks call any swampy land—a "dismal." The canal was surveyed by George Washington in 1763 and was used continuously for commercial traffic after it was completed in 1805. Ferries used it, as did barges, to carry goods from port to port. The canal is lined with trees, some of which are in bloom, and most have vines intertwined in the branches. There's that sweet smell of wild honeysuckle again. It's taken over everything along the banks, climbing up the banks and taking over the trees.

For miles it looked like we were passing through a dense jungle far from civilization. But every now and then we could see Route 17 that runs parallel to the canal for a distance. This sight brought us back to the real world. There are picnic areas along the canal where people can enjoy the canal and watch the boats pass by so closely. At the other end of the Dismal Swamp Canal there are two locks to go through, the Deep Creek Lock and the Great Bridge Lock.

We arrived at the lock at 10:00 a.m. and had to wait an hour for it to open. We had lunch while we waited.

The lock tender operated both the lock and the drawbridge, which are half a mile apart. We had to give him time to drive from one lock to the other.

We entered the Norfolk, Virginia, harbor, going under many lift bridges. The center of a lift bridge lifts up so those huge, tall navy carriers can pass through.

This harbor is an unforgettable sight. It has every type of U.S. Navy ship, from the largest aircraft carriers to sinister looking submarines. There is a replica of the "Bounty" tied up along the ICW.

The Elizabeth River goes through here with Norfolk on one side and Portsmouth on the other. There were ships being sandblasted and painted. Some were in dry dock, some were being loaded and unloaded, and some were being cut up for scrap.

In the midst of it all, scurrying up and down the harbor, were tugs, large and small, military and civilian, either pushing or pulling loaded or empty barges. There was a helicopter overhead watching the activity in the harbor. If you get out of the channel just a little bit, the coast guard patrol is right there to tell you to get back inside the channel where you belong. Security is tight!

A Young Man's Dream / An Old Man's Reality

Rodger, who had put a huge American flag on the stern of "Pockets," got out of the channel just a little. They were right there at his side ordering him to get back.

Cranes arced through the air as they handled cargo more than 100 feet above the ground. Some were as big as a two-car garage. A great variety of noises and odors accompanied all the visual activity. We couldn't even hear our own motor because of the surrounding racket. We detected an odor that smelled like hot wires, which made us check to be sure it was not our boat getting hot. In addition to contending with noises and odors, we had to listen and watch out for tugs. In a busy harbor such as this, there are boats everywhere!

Finally getting through the Norfolk harbor, we pulled into the Lafayette River to anchor for the night. A lot of debris floated through here, making it a little tricky to maneuver the boat. We had to be very careful and watch out for logs; they can cause damage to the hull. I was on it—remember that was my job. I wouldn't want to get fired!

The sun came out for a short time, but not nearly long enough. Everything in the boat was saturated from all the rain. With the ceiling dripping from condensation caused by our trying to keep the boat warm, it was like living in a shower.

"Rainbow Connection" anchored with us. Jamel radioed to Rodger to ask if he could use their computer to download pictures from his digital camera. Rodger went over in their raft to get him; but because the wind was blowing 20 mph from the wrong direction, he found it very difficult to row.

We watched and laughed at Rodger's rowing dilemma; however, it wasn't funny to Rodger. He would row, and the wind would blow him back. It was like watching a comedy show! Finally Jamel threw Rodger a rope with a fender tied on the end. He pulled Rodger close enough to be able to get in the raft. Rodger was out of steam, so Jamel rowed back to "Pockets." Luckily for Jamel, the wind was from the right direction going back. Finally everyone was back on his own boat and settled in for the night. We are no longer in the ICW.

We traveled 31.6 miles today.

Tuesday, May 20, 2003

We pulled anchor at 6:30 a.m. We had a beautiful day with very little wind as we started up the Chesapeake Bay to Wicomico River, just short of the Potomac River, near Reedville, Virginia.

To get back here, we had to pass between two huge Menhaden fishing boats, one coming in and one going out the river. We looked like a little toy boat next to those big fishing boats. You just hope that they see you, not to mention the waves they make for smaller vessels. These big ships are used for catching Menhaden fish for the cat food processing plant back here. You can imagine the odor. We were lucky the wind was blowing in the right direction. The oil from these fish is also used in cologne and lipstick.

Now in Virginia waters and going under more bridges, we passed numerous ships, coming and going in the bay. Again, we had to watch in all directions while going through here. This is another busy seaport.

Rodger and Dee will be leaving us tomorrow; they are almost home. They live in Callao, Virginia, just around the bend on up the Potomac River. They came over to visit this evening to see whether or not I am going to continue the trip with Joe.

Joe was becoming sad because he thought this would be our last night together on the boat. He was expecting me to leave with them in the morning because this is where I had said I was getting off. And I hadn't said anything different to anyone.

I had made up my mind a while back when I realized Joe couldn't do this by himself. Honestly, I couldn't see anyone else being able to put up with Joe's moods and still be friends. Several people would have liked to make the trip with him, but as Joe's wife (you know, for better or worse) I thought I should be the one sticking with him to help fulfill his dream.

To be honest, I could have pushed him overboard a time or two myself, but that's another book! Making up can be fun, and tomorrow will be a better day. We actually have had a very enjoyable and interesting trip so far. I knew that I would miss him; I wouldn't have anyone to pick on (?).

After going this far, I couldn't leave. I would be at home wondering what he was doing, where he was, and what I was missing. I think the fear of not knowing would be much worse than staying on board for the long haul.

Dee was relieved when I told her I was staying with the captain. Saying goodbye to Rodger and Dee was very emotional for all of us. We have come to love them, and we enjoyed their company every evening after dropping anchor. After lots of hugs and kisses and wiping back tears, they went back to "Pockets." We settled in for the night, not looking forward to morning, knowing we were going on without them. After traveling together for four week's, we are really going to miss them.

We have so many wonderful memories, thanks to these two; but now we must go on and make our own memories. They were very helpful, and they certainly helped me adjust to boat living in a positive way. We made a promise to stay in touch with each other. They really would like to go on with us, but they just can't. They will be taking off early in the morning. We had a very good day on the water today, but a sad evening having to say goodbye to two very nice people we have grown to love in our hearts. Well, have you already figured out that I am not going to let my husband go on by himself?

We traveled 66.9 miles today.

CHAPTER 2
NORTH - EAST:
REEDVILLE , VA .- - -TONAWANDA , NEWY

Wednesday, May 21, 2003

We were up early this morning at 6:10 a.m. It was a sad day because Rodger and Dee left us to go home. It was good for them because they are ready to be home after the ordeal of Dee's accident. It's been a rough time for her, but she's going to be fine. We already miss them. They radioed over to say goodbye and to wish us good luck. We promised to keep in touch with them as we continue on The Great Circle. I was choking back tears, so Joe did all the talking.

At 8:00 we radioed to "Rainbow Connection" to see what they were planning to do. They needed fuel. A marina located just around the bend in the harbor sold fuel, so we went there and waited for them to open. It was 10:00 a.m. by the time they were refueled, causing us to get a late start this morning.

Running with the Canadians, we started up the Chesapeake with a south wind. The radio was predicting the wind would change to the north and get stronger. Three-foot waves were coming at us making the boat pitch (rock back and forth) like a bucking horse. I thought Joe had hit his head one too many times going through the boat's companionway when he yelled, "Yahoo! Ride 'em cowboy!" I told him he was crazy.

We radioed to "Rainbow Connection" to tell them we were heading for an anchorage just ahead. They radioed back to say they were going on; they had a deadline to get back to Canada and had to keep going or they would not make it on time. A few minutes later Don radioed back to say he had had enough and was coming in also. Don did not have inside steering on his boat, and he was taking a beating from the wind and rain.

It was raining so hard we could barely see them coming up behind us. We had to stay in contact by radio. Their hand-held does not have a very strong signal, but we kept in touch long enough to get into a safe anchorage. It is good to have a GPS, which shows your position on a map. You simply follow the passage on the screen to go where you want to go.

The rain and wind caused us to toss around like a toy boat. We took them up the Patuxant River and anchored in Mill Creek just outside Solomon's Islands, Maryland. We were glad to get back here in a calm anchorage for the night.

We radioed to "Rainbow Connection" to check in with them and to make sure they were okay. They said they were fine and we would give it a go again in the morning. It was really getting nasty; we got back here at just the right time. It's 6:00 p.m., and we are anchored in a safe place for the night. God is watching over us.

We traveled 52.7 miles today.

Thursday, May 22, 2003

We got up this morning to find that "Rainbow Connection" was gone. They must have waited for the storm to pass and then headed out. We tried reaching them by radio. We knew they were on a deadline to get back to Canada by June 1, but we wish we could have told them goodbye. Don had said they would have to continue all night to make their deadline. Joe and I had already decided we were not going to travel at night. To me it is dangerous; and, besides, you would miss all the sights. The Canadians make this trip every spring like a lot of northerners do.

The weather was still cloudy and rainy. We decided to go into a marina, get hooked up to some electric, get a shower, do some laundry, and hope the weather would get better.

Going into Solomon's Islands, Maryland, across Back Creek, we got a slip at the Beacon Marina for the weekend. This is just across the creek from where we were last night.

Even though it was still misting rain, we showered, walked to town, and ate at a Roy Rogers Hardee's restaurant. Joe wanted a $6 burger, but this was a chicken Hardee's and we ate chicken!

There is a strip mall here where we found a grocery and other interesting stores. At a West Marine we bought matching warm, blue fleece sweaters on sale (a good deal); they were perfect for this weather. Joe bought an all-weather windbreaker, and I found that rain suit he promised me (yellow). So now when we have to lock through, I will look like a big yellow duck; but at least I will stay dry. I sure don't want to get sick.

We walked back to the boat loaded down with all our purchases. It was damp and cold. We could use the little electric heater we left back in Ft. Myers, thinking we wouldn't need it on this trip. The weather has been unpleasant ever since we separated from Rodger and Dee. I think the Angels are sad they didn't come with us; so are we. We miss their company with Rodger's wit and Dee's sweet smile.

At the marina office we heard there is going to be an air show this weekend with the Blue Angels performing if the weather cooperates. This will be an event that will be fun to watch from the cockpit of our boat.

We didn't make any miles today. We went from being anchored in the creek to the marina across the cove. We hope it stops raining so the Blue Angels can fly tomorrow.

Saturday, May 24, 2003

We woke up to a cloudy day with a promise of clear skies by afternoon. The Calvert Marine Museum is located right behind the marina; we decided to walk over there to check it out.

What a great decision! This is an interesting museum, with lots of marine history from old boats to antique marine motors and all kinds of sea life in aquariums. We actually watched a sea horse having babies! They also have an otter in a pool; he will show off for anyone who would stand there to watch him. He would dive and float on his back and make sounds to keep your attention. There were fossils and jaws of teeth from sharks of all sizes on display. Old Indian canoes were displayed. Displays explaining Indian life in the early days included information about crafts, clothing, and hunting tools. We both love Indian history and found all this fascinating.

The oldest coast-guard-licensed passenger-carrying vessel in the Chesapeake, "The William B. Tennison" is docked here.

One of only three remaining cottage style lighthouses that served at the turn of the century, the Drum Point Lighthouse, has been restored to its original appearance. The octagon shaped lighthouse is up on eight pilings with a stairway leading to the first floor, which is divided like a pie. Then another stairway leads to the top floor where there are bedrooms. A light and bell used to warn sailors of danger in bad weather are on this floor. It is hard to believe that families lived and worked in these compact lighthouses years ago. They must not have been very big people or they couldn't have gotten up the stairway. It was a tight squeeze for me.

After this, we walked back into town to get some groceries and a hair dryer. I plan to use the hair dryer to put some warm air in the boat and to dry my hair at the same time. I hope it stops raining one of these days. Thank goodness, we have God's promise of the rainbow because it seems like it's been raining for 40 days and 40 nights.

Hurrah!! The sun came out and the air show with the Blue Angels was spectacular. They, along with other aircraft, went right over our boat.

Today is the Captain's 66th birthday. I took the still good-looking captain over to the Captain's Table restaurant here at the marina for a birthday dinner. Wearing our matching blue fleece sweaters, we walked to the restaurant early in order to beat the crowd. There's been a crowd every night since we have been here, so we thought the food must be good.

Joe ordered the Seafood Platter Special. I ordered the Jumbo Shrimp with onion rings and salad. Both of us had their raspberry iced tea. Now we know why it was crowded every night. The food was delicious!

Celebrating the "Captain's Birthday"

We asked our waitress to take a picture to record this special day of our journey. We had a great day together!

Sunday, May 25, 2003

We started out this morning, the first day alone, with just the Admiral and her Captain. It was a little foggy, cold, and 60 degrees. We had a beam sea (wind coming at us from the side, making us rock sideways) out to Chesapeake Bay. The marine radio reported a large barge had hit a fishing boat. Since no one was found around the boat, everyone in the area was asked to be on the lookout for survivors out in the water. A number of boats were helping by keeping the area marked off to keep anyone from going too close to the accident. Thank goodness, we didn't see anyone floating!

The sun came out for a little while, but the day was mostly cloudy. We traveled for miles not seeing anything but water and hundreds of fishing boats trolling with poles hanging any place they could put one. It was like an obstacle course going through them. We were told the fishing boats have the right of way in the water, and we just wove our way around them very carefully. There are serious fishermen around here.

We anchored in Lake Ogleton at the mouth of the Severn River close to Annapolis, Maryland, at 2:30 p.m. It was a gloomy day on the water, but together we made it without any problems. Just the two of us (yeah)!

Joe changed the oil and filter.

We traveled 54.6 miles.

Monday, May 26, 2003 (Memorial Day)

The weather was too bad to travel today, so we stayed anchored in Lake Ogleton. Joe changed the fuel filters and I tried to get the boat dried out. We haven't had enough dry air to be able to open up the boat long enough for it to dry out; it doesn't take long for the mold to take over.

The sun came out about 4:30 just enough to tease us, but we did see some blue skies for a few hours. Maybe our bad luck with the weather is changing. On days like this you just chill out and make the best of it, trying to get caught up on things you aren't able do while you are underway and hope tomorrow will be a better day for boating.

In an 11 by 31 foot boat, you have to hug to pass in the hallway. That could make for a fun chapter (if you know what I mean).

It has been so damp and cold that we can't open up the windows or companionway door.

Today has not given much of interest to write about. Maybe tomorrow will be better. This is a true test of togetherness!!

Tuesday, May 27, 2003

Having had our coffee, we pulled anchor at 7:30 a.m. Hurray! We have sunshine. We headed out of the Severn River to Chesapeake Bay.

We went under more big bridges, one of which was The William P. Lane Memorial. We passed the Sharps Island Lighthouse.

These old lighthouses out here in the bay are so awesome with their foghorns sounding and their beams of light shining across the water to warn sailors of danger. They have been a welcome sight for many a sailor for decades.

We had calm water all day with only a little fog and light wind. A light sprinkle about 3:00 was enough to make us steer from inside.

We anchored at Chesapeake City on the C&D (Chesapeake and Delaware) Canal at 4:30 p.m. There are stores and restaurants back in this cove. We could hear good country music coming from one of them while we sat in the cockpit of the boat. We had a nice relaxing evening with lots of ducks swimming around us for entertainment. The only thing better would be blue skies with big puffy white clouds in the morning! We had another good day.

We traveled 57.7 miles today.

Wednesday, May 28, 2003

We pulled anchor at 8:40 a.m. after a restful night. We were two hours away from Delaware Bay. With the promise of a calm day, we decided to head for the Cohansey River. This would make a 40-mile day for us. The tide was with us, letting us make really good time. Everything was going well. When we got to the entrance of the river where we had planned to stop for the day, we decided to go on to Cape May, New Jersey. Since the weather was good and we still had a lot of daytime left, we could get in a few more miles before stopping.

I watched eight seagulls flying right behind us, diving down into the water, catching fish, and then coming back up. It looked like they were trying to come into the cockpit or land on top of the bimini. They did a lot of squawking and flew behind us for miles. I sat out in the cockpit watching and trying to get a picture of them. It was quite a sight.

We were going along, having a good day, passing the only anchorage where we could stop, when the weather suddenly turned bad and it started raining hard. Then we looked behind us to see a huge ocean freighter, fully loaded with stacks of cargo container's from trains, going full speed and getting ready to pass us. Coming at us was a wave big enough to swallow us

Joe looked at me with fear in his eyes and said, "Hurry, lock the companionway door and hang on; this is going to be bad." I just barely had time to get the door locked and back to my seat to say a prayer.

WHAM!! The huge wave hit us, and we went airborne ten feet in the air. About two thirds of the boat went up in the air; and, SLAM; we hit the water like a ton of bricks on cement. The sound of the boat hitting the water was horrifying. I just held on to my seat and prayed to God that the boat would stay in one piece and not crack open like an egg.

We looked at each other totally stunned. Then Joe said, "Check the bilge and see if we are taking on any water." I checked, and everything down there looked good. Joe had to make a fast decision about which way to point the boat—to have the stern or the bow facing the big wave of water coming at us. I think Joe made the right decision by turning the bow out so the water went over the windshield and the pilothouse rather than coming into the cockpit, the companionway door, and the pilothouse. He's still not sure he did the right thing, but I think he did. He thinks we would have ridden out the wave if we had turned and steered away from it. Then it would have pushed us forward instead of hitting us head on. Through hindsight, I think he did the right thing. I hope we never have to make that decision again. We both sent up a big "thank you" prayer to God.

With the motor still running, Joe put her in gear and on we went, shook up, but thankful we were still in one piece. Everything seemed to be working okay.

On down the Delaware Bay we went. The American flag was whipping in the wind and rain. This was not fun. The white caps on the water threw the boat around, tossing me all over the boat. I hung on tightly so I wouldn't slam into the galley stove or the counter. We were being tossed around badly.

Joe decided after a few miles of this that he had had enough. Checking the GPS, he decided to leave the channel and take a shortcut across the bay to get in smoother water. This was a good decision. With the wind on the stern, the boat rode a lot more smoothly. We had missed three big freighters over in the channel. Just seeing one of those big freighters made both of us panic.

We motored past the Ship-John Shoal Lighthouse out in the middle of Delaware Bay. The foghorn was sounding to warn boaters of danger. I wish we had had a warning about that big freighter! We could see big boulders that we needed to stay clear of in the shoal water surrounding the lighthouse.

Looking in all directions, we saw nothing but water, water, and more water. I remember someone telling me that we would never lose sight of land (wrong). I could not see any land at this time, and this was a bit scary. We had gone for quite a while out in the open water.

I asked Joe if he was watching for a dove with a fig leaf in its mouth to find us. Now I know how Noah felt looking for land. It was a very good feeling when we finally saw trees and land on the horizon.

Finally, LAND HO!!!

We set course for Cape May, New Jersey, and anchored just off to the side of the ICW at 7:00 p.m. coming into Cape May, we saw ferry transport ships that will take you across the bay. They look like triple-decker ships. Very impressive!

We were exhausted and still in a daze from the horrible incident with the freighter and were thankful to be anchored for the night out of the Delaware Bay.

We traveled 77.1 miles.

Thursday, May 29, 2003

We slept in this morning, still trying to recuperate from yesterday's ordeal. Joe is still bragging about the boat's staying together. At 10:00 a.m. we pulled anchor and headed back into the ICW to go up the Jersey coast.

On the ICW we saw narrow barrier islands between it and the Atlantic Ocean. It was really a spectacular sight to look across the islands and see the Atlantic, a huge body of blue-green water as far as you can see. I can't imagine trying to cross it in our boat, but I know people do this every day.

The houses along the Jersey shore are built so close together that they look like they are attached to one another. They continue for miles and miles along the shoreline. Most homes are three stories high and are built right over the water. This permits owners to drive right into their water garages and be home. This is a wonderful idea for those living on the ICW.

Going through Ocean City, we encountered fishermen in the middle of the channel who didn't even offer to move out of the way; we had to go around them. However, this did help us locate the channel; we just had to maneuver our way around them because "they be doin' some serious fishin' here."

Everyone around here fishes; there is not a spot in the water that does not have a boat of some sort in it. There must have been thousands of boats; they were everywhere we looked.

We had to have two bridges raised for us. I think we woke up the bridge tender with our air horn. He finally raised the bridge enough for us to go under it, and we called back to thank him. We could have blown the air horn to let him know we were through. After the boat passes under the bridge, it is lowered for traffic to pass over it.

We anchored at 5:45 p.m. for the night in Ventnor City, New Jersey in a quiet harbor back in a small cove. Believe me, we were ready to relax and enjoy a calm, quiet anchorage. We had a good day, but we are still shook up over our experience with the freighter.

We traveled 44.4 miles today.

Friday, May 30, 2003

We enjoyed our morning coffee on this nice sunny day after having a good breakfast. We left our anchorage at 11:00 a.m. This was a late start; we were still trying to recuperate after the big ship nightmare.

It takes a lot out of you to be at the wheel all day, to stay in the channel watching for both floating debris and other boats crossing your path, and to keep a constant watch in every direction. I help by watching and by keeping track of the navigational markers that Joe has difficulty seeing. He gets a little testy with me once in a while, and I have to bite my tongue and let him vent his frustration. Every now and then he just needs to stop and rest a little (me too!).

We passed more homes that appear to be built on top of each other. Neighbors living this close would certainly have to get along with one another. No space is wasted through here for trees or grass; water comes almost to the front door. I find it interesting that they live right on top of the waterway and I wonder if all the moisture affects things inside. Maybe everything is made from PVC pipe and plastic.

Today we were finally able to open up the boat to let some fresh warm air through it, and it was wonderful! Maybe I can finally get this place dried out. I actually sat out in the cockpit in the warm sun and took some pictures. I haven't been able to do that for a while. It was nice to sit out today, soaking up sunshine and warming up my bones.

We went past Atlantic City, New Jersey. Beyond a railroad track on shore, we could see the Trump Plaza and Casino and Harrah's Casino from the waterway.

After going through Atlantic City and past the beaches, we ran into some shallow water and had to churn our way through sand and mud. Again, we are glad to have that extra horsepower. The blue chip on the GPS wasn't up to date and had us taking an old route, which was not open for navigation any longer. Not knowing this, we took off through that route. I think we opened it again with the propeller churning slowly through the sand. We finally made it back over to the right route (I think).

Finally we were back in the right channel going through the Great Bay, which is nothing compared to the Delaware Bay, and into Little Egg Harbor. Joe says we should have crossed on a high tide instead of a rising tide, but we made it. We called ahead to Beach Haven Marina in Beach Haven, New Jersey, for a reservation because more bad weather was being forecast. We don't need any more rain; I'm beginning to prune up.

Getting to the marina at 3:30 p.m., we pulled up to the fuel dock to fill up with diesel fuel. The young man in charge of the dock was from Hawaii. Mai (pronounced "May"), along with another man named George, welcomed us to the marina.

George, his wife, and their two school aged daughters have lived on a sailboat here at the marina for 26 years. He told us they had built their boat. Joe was impressed; it was a rather large sailboat. The wind was starting to pick up, so the men helped us get the boat tied to the dock and explained how to get to town from the marina. George even offered us his car if we needed one, but we needed to get some exercise and town was only a few blocks away.

By the time we got to town the stores were closed, but we had a nice stroll through town. Finding a few restaurants still open, we stopped at Fred's Beach Haven Diner. I ordered the perfectly grilled pork chops, baked potato, peas and carrots, and a bowl of chunky tomato soup (I was stuffed); Joe had a Mexican plate dinner. It was good food at a reasonable price.

On the say back to the boat we found some stores we would come back to check out tomorrow. We stopped at the grocery store for milk, got the local paper, and headed back to the boat ready to get a good night's sleep. It is interesting to see how the people in these little towns along the waterway live. Of course, they all decorate with sea ornaments and seashells. Some don't even have grass; their yards are crushed seashells. A variety of cactus grows in their yards. I'm sure a lot of the homes are seasonal.

We traveled 26 miles today.

Saturday, May 31, 2003

We are still docked at Beach Haven, New Jersey. We woke up to a sunny morning, had coffee and breakfast, and walked back to town. Oh, it was nice to get off the boat and walk! We needed to get some warm clothing because it is getting chilly in the evenings. I got a pair of knit pants and a Beach Haven T-shirt to take back home to one of the kids for a Christmas gift.

We found a store that develops pictures in one hour, and I had four rolls to drop off. I'm always anxious to see how they turn out because the boat is always rocking when I'm taking a picture. I'm amazed they turn out as good as they do.

While we were waiting for the pictures to be developed, we walked three blocks to the Atlantic Ocean and sat on a bench on the beach and watched the waves roll in. Those waves were rolling in fast and furiously from the storm we could see coming in from the east.

All the houses along the beach have sand piled up with layers of fencing to keep the sand from eroding and to help stop the water from coming all the way to the house during a storm. We saw a man fishing and a few other hardy souls out on the beach. The wind was picking up and dark storm clouds were rolling across the sky. It started to sprinkle on us as we hurried back to the film shop, picked up the film, and headed down the street. When it started raining harder, we dashed into a department store to wait it out and to look around. I purchased a cute outfit there for myself, so it wasn't a total waste of time.

The rain stopped long enough for us to get down to A Slice of Haven Pizza for a snack. On the way back to the boat, we stopped at a bookstore to pick up some reading material; I'm always looking for a good book. We stopped at the store to pick up some Coke for Joe and then headed back to the boat just in time before the rain came pouring down again.

Tornado warnings were out for this area, and it was getting foggy and nasty. We are glad we are docked at a marina. It was too nasty to go back out, so we heated some soup for dinner and then called friends back home we haven't talked to in a while.

We called Rodger and Dee, Josh and Rachel, Jack and Kathy, John and Judy, Mark and Trish; it's always good to hear a friendly voice. We are pleased that our friends are interested in our journey, and some are even keeping track of us on the map. It is fun to report back to them every other week or so on the cell phone.

We've been gone 43 days on the boat and five months from Shoals, Indiana; it seems like forever.

We have the marine radio turned on in order to stay on top of weather conditions. It doesn't sound very promising for being on the water for the next few days. I wonder how long we are going to have to stay here. The good news is that we are not far from town, and they have laundry facilities here.

Sunday, June 1, 2003

We are still docked at Beach Haven; the weather is not fit for either land or sea. It is rainy and foggy, the wind is blowing 40 knots, tornado warnings are still being issued, and the sky looks really angry. Breaking waves have been coming in against the docks all day. I have been reading a book I got from the bookstore in town, and Joe has moved the location of the autopilot. The rain has finally let up a little, but not the wind.

We took showers and did the laundry today as soon as the rain let up long enough that we wouldn't get soaked leaving the boat.

We walked to town to Fred's Diner again, and we both ordered the Mexican plate dinner. We also picked up some groceries just in case we can't get to town tomorrow.

We returned to the boat; it was still foggy and raining. We heard the roar of engines and could see dozens of racing "cigar" boats go past, and we wondered where in the world they could be going in this weather. It was so foggy you couldn't see and it was raining. These boats are all open; we know they are getting soaked. It doesn't look like fun to us. We think they are all nuts!

Later they all went back. With their big horse-powered motors, they could be heard coming for miles; they are powerful boats.

Getting ready for bed, we could hear the wind blowing hard and feel it jerking the boat back and forth. With the sound of the whistling wind and the ropes being pulled in all directions, it seems like the boat is being pulled apart even though we are tied to the dock pilings. I hate that sound; it is scary and I can't sleep. Of course, Joe is snoozing like an old bear. I'll be glad to see morning; I don't like the boat rocking and jerking around like this. I did finally fall asleep around 3:00 a.m. I was glad to see morning come and see we are still in one piece, but the wind is still blowing and rocking us around badly. Joe doesn't like it either, but there's not much we can do other than wait it out.

Monday, June 2, 2003

After getting through the restless night and thinking we were tied up in a safe marina, we found the wind was coming in from the wrong direction causing us to toss around. Joe decided that it couldn't be any worse out on the river (scary thought).

At 9:15 we headed out of the Beach Haven Marina. The water was still a little choppy, but the sun was shining and it was a rather nice day. Tied up to the dock, we were being jerked back and forth because we were taking the wind on the beam (from the side). Once we left, we had a great day on the water. It was 82 degrees today. This was another good decision made by the Captain. We traveled past more beautiful homes, but we still saw no trees anywhere. It's really strange not to see trees in the yards.

We went up Crabtown Creek through the Point Pleasant Canal and anchored at 4:10 p.m. in Glimmer Glass, a cove off the main channel. It is the most beautiful and peaceful place we have experienced recently. After Beach Haven, it is nice to find this relaxing spot.

As we were throwing out the anchor, two big swans greeted us as they swam past the boat. I jokingly asked, "You guys want a cracker?" They turned around, made a beeline to the boat, and started talking to me. I think they understood me. When they saw I didn't actually have crackers in my hand, they proceeded to hiss their dissatisfaction. I got some crackers right away and fed them.

Joe and I sat out in the cockpit watching the swans and enjoying the calm water. We ended up having a wonderful day with a beautiful sunset here at Glimmer Glass. This enjoyable stop is a must for anyone making a trip to this locality.

We are only eight miles from the Atlantic Ocean. We will soon leave the ICW and travel the Atlantic for about 30 miles. Joe is a bit apprehensive about this.

We traveled 45.2 miles today.

Tuesday, June 3, 2003

This morning we woke up to bright, wonderful sunshine. Joe had a cup of coffee ready and waiting for me.

We heard commuter trains going past all evening. Obviously, people use them extensively for traveling to work, to go shopping, etc., judging by the number of trains we saw. This is another aspect of how people live differently in our country.

The friendly swans were back for breakfast, and I treated them to a slice of bread at 6:45 before we headed out to the Atlantic Ocean. We were in the Atlantic today for about 30 miles, headed to Sandy Hook, New Jersey.

This took about five hours.

The ICW ends at Mannasquan, New Jersey, making it necessary to go out in the Atlantic if you want to continue; otherwise, you turn around and go back. We have been apprehensive about the Atlantic because it seems to be too intimidating for a sailboat like ours. We could see small fishing boats out there, but they looked like they were going to be swallowed up by the waves. Nevertheless, we went ahead like we knew what we were doing.

It turned out to be a perfectly wonderful sunny day. The calm water was gorgeous with hues of blue and green; the beautiful blue sky made for a perfect day. The waves were just a constant smooth up and down movement that was relaxing and enjoyable. If only all water could be this smooth! Our apprehensions were put to rest; we just needed to have a little faith!

We planned to stop at the Atlantic Highlands, New Jersey, across the bay from Sandy Hook, to visit our good friends Mark and Trish.

We arrived at the Highlands about noon and called Mark, who informed us he was working at the Keyport Yacht Club in Keyport, New Jersey. He told us to come up there because he could get us a mooring (a ball out in the water to which you hook your boat).

To get to Keyport, we had to go back to Sandy Hook Bay, which we had just come through. We again had to dodge the many commercial fishing boats that were fishing for blue fish. We also were in Raritan Bay before arriving at Keyport at 2:00. The weather was beginning to get nasty again, so we got there just in time.

Mark met us in the harbor in the launch, which is a boat used to taxi people back and forth from the marina dock to their boat. He came aboard and visited with us for a while. He had to get back to work, but he came back to check on us before leaving work to go home. We told him we were fine and we would see him tomorrow. We invited him to come by when he was out on the launch.

It was good to see Mark and we can't wait to see Trish. They are the greatest, most fun loving couple you could ever meet. I could write a whole chapter on just those two.

We traveled 50.2 miles today.

Wednesday, June 4, 2003

The 20-25 knot winds kept me up most of the night. The rain poured down and the boat pitched and rolled all night, never letting up. This just about did me in this time. I thought I was going to get sick from the constant jerking of the boat; it just wouldn't let up. The mooring harbor here is open toward the east, so the wind off the Raritan Bay comes right in. With no seawalls or anything for protection, the wind caused the boat to swing around, pitching up and down and back and forth constantly. It was as though someone was shaking it with all his might. This was worse than going airborne; at least that didn't last long. It compared to being in an agitating washing machine. It was not good.

Mark came out to the boat this morning to tell us to get a few things together; we were going to stay in their home tonight. I was so happy to see him that I could have kissed him! Just getting off the boat would help. We grabbed a few things and boarded the launch. I didn't know Trish was waiting in the car; it was so good to see her smiling face.

After getting to their home, Mark fixed some hot tea, which helped settle my stomach. It was still in a big knot from the night before.

After visiting a while and settling my nerves with tea, we went out to eat at the Grand Chinese Buffet. We ate too much, but it was so good. Afterwards, Mark took us to visit his brother and sister-in-law, Bob and Ann, in their lovely home. We had a wonderful time visiting with them, and they wanted to hear all about our trip. I never realized that so many people were interested in making a trip like this.

After leaving Bob and Ann, Mark drove us around town to see some of it. Then he took us out to Sandy Hook Beach to show us the famous lighthouse there. However, we couldn't see very far because of the rain and fog so we headed back to their house.

Trish put in a Kevin Costner movie, opened a bottle of wine, and then opened her snack closet. Her stash of snacks is unbelievable; the closet has shelves from top to bottom stocked with every snack imaginable. This lady is prepared for a party at any time.

In their living room there was an extra long sofa with one end curved that was perfect for curling up to watch TV in front of the fireplace. They made us feel right at home. It was good not to be rocking and rolling in our boat, but instead resting here in their comfortable home.

We are so thankful for the wonderful people who have become our friends because of our boating contacts and experiences. We appreciate their opening their home and hearts to us. Thank you, Mark and Trish, for your friendship and your hospitality—we think the world of you!

Thursday June 5, 2003

Mark fixed us a very nutritious, breakfast this morning. Along with a good cup of coffee, we had oatmeal with raisins and a delicious English muffin with peanut butter and jelly. Now every time we have oatmeal we will think of Mark.

Mark took us back to our boat even though it's still too foggy to take the boat out. They wanted us to stay. Tomorrow promises to be a great day, and we want to be ready if the weather window is there. We want to be up early and on the boat ready to go, weather permitting.

When Mark came to work at 4:00, he came out to the boat and loaned us his car so we could go to the grocery and run some errands. He gave us directions for getting around town. After running our errands, we stopped for a hamburger. We bought a beautiful red mini-rosebush for Trish for being such a gracious hostess and put gas in Mark's car before returning it. They are such super nice people!

We returned to the boat to get ready to continue our journey north tomorrow, weather permitting. We listened to the marine radio, and it sounded like conditions would be good.

I could easily have stayed here, but we can't finish the trip if we don't keep going and staying on schedule. So, we are ready to go if the weather is a go!

Friday, June 6, 2003

We woke up at 6:00 a.m. to a beautiful sunrise, no rain, no wind, and no fog. New York, here we come!

We left Keyport Yacht Club with our mugs of coffee and a 10-knot wind. We made our way out of Raritan Bay and across the Lower New York Bay, getting across with no problems and no freighters, thank God!

We went under the Verazanno Narrows Bridge into upper New York Harbor where there were many BIG freighters in the middle of the harbor, some loading and some unloading cargo onto smaller ships. This is a very busy harbor with dozens of water taxis, including the Staten Island Ferry, which is a big vessel that hauls commuters back and forth from the Island to Manhattan all day long. With all the water taxi traffic, which keeps the harbor churned up, it was not easy going through there. It would have been easier to cross on Sunday when the water taxis don't run, but we would have lost two more days and we couldn't wait. Live and learn!

The Manhattan skyline is exciting when seen from the water, and then there is the Statue of Liberty on Liberty Island. AWESOME! AWESOME!

The sight of Lady Liberty holding the torch over her head, welcoming all vessels into the upper bay, gave us chills. It must be a wonderful sight to see her lit up at night. Seeing the statue made the trip through the bay worthwhile. On up the river, past the statue, we saw the Main Building on Ellis Island where the immigrants came in. A beautiful building, it is now a museum.

Across the bay from the statue was the navy aircraft carrier, "Intrepid." The deck was loaded with tomcats, helicopters, and other aircraft. Several other battleships were also docked along here.

Tall buildings stretched across the skyline. The cruise ship, "Carnival Legend," was in the upper bay. We moved slowly through here; the tide was against us, and we had to dodge all the other boats. The New York water taxis zipped back and forth, keeping the water churned up and making for a rough passage. With all this tossing around, I hope my pictures turn out well.

After getting past the East River, we got up to 5 mph. We saw the big sign on top of a building that spelled "YONKERS," and we passed many old docks and warehouses in a sad state of repair. There were factories, which were once busy producing textiles. Behind these are the many high-rise buildings that form the downtown Manhattan area. Gradually these tall buildings give way to the smaller apartment buildings seen as you cruise north up the Hudson River.

Some racing sailboats passed us as we went up the Hudson River. As we went under the George Washington Bridge we lost sight of the city, but New York's country area came into view. The river became calmer as we moved up it, and the view along here was absolutely beautiful.

Railroad tracks, just a few feet above water level, were on both sides of the river. From our point of view, trains on the tracks looked like they were skimming across the water. On one side we noticed commuter trains and freight trains on the other. Tunnels for the trains were cut through the solid rock of the mountainsides. It was quite a sight to see a train disappear and then reappear through the tunnel on the other side of the mountain.

The trees on the hills made a solid green covering, with a few houses appearing among the trees now and then. I wondered where the roads leading to them were located. It is really beautiful through here, but there is no place to anchor along here because the water is so deep and the banks are composed of rock.

We went under the Tappen Zee Bridge and past Sing-Sing Prison. We saw tugs pushing barges past us; some had as many as ten or more barges tied together. It's amazing how those tugs maneuver the barges through the deep water and around the bends in the river.

We moved through Haverstraw Bay, passed Sleepy Hollow, and saw more tree-covered hills—miles of them. There were places where rocks showed through on the mountainside.

One of the mountain ranges through here is called Big Bear. I wondered if there are bears up there.

We passed the United States Military Academy, West Point, over on the west bank. Visitors are welcome and could even spend the night and take a tour of the Academy. It is an impressive place to see from the water, especially at night when it is lit up.

There is an old foundry along here where cannons were made during the Civil War. There is so much history to learn about through here if only there was time to stop and explore. That could be another whole trip in itself!

Because it was getting late, we began looking for a place to drop anchor for the night. Joe had read about an island with the ruins of a castle on it somewhere through here. If we could find it, we thought it would be an interesting place to anchor if we could find it before dark. Then, too, there would have to be enough water behind the castle for us to anchor.

At 6:45 we saw the Pollepel Island with the ruins of a full size castle on it. It was upriver a little ways, but we finally got in behind it after a couple of tries. The water was fairly shallow back there, but the captain got us in safely.

I wish we could have gotten on the island to see the castle up close. The island was overgrown with trees and weeds, but we could still see quite a bit of this awesome castle. We could make out the four-foot-high letters around the top that read "Bannerman's Island Arsenal." With its turrets, parapets, crenellations, and battlements that could be seen through the trees, it looked like something from <u>Tales of the Knights of the Round Table</u> or <u>Romeo and Juliet.</u> Joe said my imagination was working overtime. Out in the water were pillars that could have been used to hold the drawbridge or to form the moat that once surrounded the castle. I was fascinated by all of this. I was curious about it and hoped to find out more about this castle fortress.

On shore behind us was the train track that we have seen all along the foothills. We heard the commuter trains all night long. They run just as fast going backward as they do going forward.

We had a very good night while anchored back behind the castle. This was our longest day on the water so far.

We traveled 78.8 miles.

Saturday, June 7, 2003

We pulled anchor at 9:30 a.m. after a nice quiet night perfect for sleeping. As we worked our way out to the Hudson River, we looked back at the mysterious castle. We could now see the other side of it; with the green hills in the background, it was a beautiful sight. I hope the beauty of this place comes through in the pictures I took.

On the bank we could see where dynamite had been put into the rocks to blast away the hillside, making it possible to build the railroad tracks. There is so much history along this stretch of water!

Going past Newburgh, New York, where George Washington had his headquarters, we could see many old churches with their tall steeples rising above the trees.

It started raining and becoming foggy. The farther up the river we went, the worse the fog grew, making it hard to navigate. The map on the blue chip in the GPS ran out, and we had to navigate by the map-tech chart. We had to navigate by the channel markers; fortunately, the river through here is deep, making the whole river the channel. We had to be careful not to hit the trash and junk that floated in the river.

We caught a rising tide and were able to go from 5 mph to 7 mph. Spring rains have kept the water deeper than usual. Although we were making good time running up stream with a rising tide, we decided that with the thick fog coming in it was getting too dangerous to stay out here. We couldn't see the markers, so we pulled into Rondout Creek outside Kingston, New York, and went four miles up the creek. We anchored for the night at 4:30.

While moving up the creek, we passed an old wreck just rusting in the water along the bank. A big tree had fallen along the bank, making a good perch for birds and a haven for fish. We passed an adorable little sandstone cottage; trimmed in aqua, it had a spire on the roof. Pink rose bushes bloomed in front of the cottage, which looked like a big dollhouse.

Stopping here was a good decision; it will be a peaceful, safe anchorage for the night. Joe has done well at getting us into good anchorages. Rodger would be proud of him.

We traveled 39.3 miles today.

Sunday, June 8, 2003

We woke up this morning after having a very good night's rest. I fixed eggs and grits with coffee. We pulled anchor at 10:00 a.m., went past the old Kingston Lighthouse, and headed back out to the Hudson River. There was no fog; it looked like it would be a good day.

Farther up the Hudson we saw another old lighthouse at Esopus Creek. The lighthouses on the Hudson all look like cottages out on the water's edge. These beautiful old buildings are still in remarkably good shape; but they are either abandoned or turned into museums, which is a good idea since they are in such good shape.

While going up the river today, we saw some beautiful country, mostly lush green countryside with hills off in the distance. A few homes, nestled among trees, dotted the hillsides.

We went against the current all day at 5 mph, making for a slow day. We saw dozens of swans out in the river; the Catskill Mountains to the west formed a backdrop for them, making a picture-perfect scene. The sky became a bit cloudy as we went under the Rip Van Winkle Bridge and past Sleepy Hollow Lake. There are many storybook titles all along the Hudson. More tugs and barges slowly moved by us as we made our way up the river.

We went through the town of Hudson on the Hudson. Painted on one side of a building, a huge colorful mural advertising the town caught our attention.

An old home overlooking the river from the side of a high hill certainly has a magnificent view of the river. The hills are farther away from the river here, and more flat land with farms along the riverbanks can be seen.

We tried to anchor behind Rattlesnake Island, but it was too shallow. After almost hanging up in the shallow water, we crossed the creek and anchored behind Coxsackie Island at 5:40 p.m.

The sun came out just in time to set. We heard Canada geese overhead, but couldn't see them. "Now, this is boating!" as Rodger would say. We have another good anchorage and had a good day on the river.

We traveled 38.7 miles today.

Monday, June 9, 2003

Pulling anchor at 9:00 a.m., we finally left on a rising tide. As we left the anchorage, a pair of Canada geese was taking six little goslings out for a morning swim. They were so cute! It was cloudy, but there was no rain. We saw cranes, instead of seagulls, along the banks here.

We saw homes that were quite elaborate as we went through Albany, New York, the capital of the state. There were many old industrial warehouses through here, and the tall buildings were the first we had seen since leaving New York City. It looked like we were getting back into civilization.

As we passed through Albany, we saw hundreds of big petroleum tanks along the river. We saw the "Capt. J. P.," a paddlewheel tour boat from Fort Myers, Florida, as we went under the Dunn Memorial Bridge, the first bridge in downtown Albany. "Capt. J. P." must have been here working on the Hudson River.

Waving back to the people on board the "Capt. J. P.," we dropped back behind it and went on up the Hudson to Troy, New York. The closer we got to Troy, the stronger the current became. A south wind of 15 mph made the Hudson very choppy and steering was difficult. The heavy spring rains have flooded the rivers, making navigation more difficult than usual.

At Troy we went through the first locks; we went up 16 feet. This is a federal lock, operated by the U.S. government and is the first lock of the New York canal system.

We arrived at Waterford, New York, at 1:30 p.m. Many boats were tied up here waiting to go through the locks. This is where we would start through the Erie Canal. We needed to find a spot to tie up along the wall; then we would go to the Waterford City Visitors Center to check in.

While checking for information about the town at the information table, I found a magazine with a picture of the castle on Pollepel Island. I couldn't believe it! An article in it told about the castle's interesting history. I was thrilled to find this because I had been so fascinated by the castle and wanted to know more about it.

The showers are free for all boaters, so we took showers and walked to town to get our first original New York Pizza. Getting past the New York accent, we ordered our pizza. It was delicious.

We walked across town, walking off some of the pizza in the process, and then crossed the bridge that goes over the Hudson to Troy. We bought some groceries and browsed through a dollar store. When we left the store, we discovered that a light rain shower had gone through. The sun had come out, and we saw the most beautiful rainbow. Joe and I commented, "God is giving us a sign of good times ahead."

After making our way back to the marina, our arms loaded with groceries, we relaxed out in the cockpit. We watched people walking with their kids and dogs. It's fun to watch people. Dozens of Canada geese and goslings have made their home here; they are cute, but noisy, critters. This was a good day!

We traveled 30.5 miles today.

Tuesday, June 10, 2003

We woke up to a beautiful day in Waterford. The sun was shining, and we were able to open up the boat and I have just chilled out on the boat today, watching people, looking at boats, and enjoying the day. We filled the water tanks, getting ready to leave in the morning. Now, this is boating!

At 5:00 we walked to town to have dinner and ended up at Kielty's Emerald Isle, an Irish pub. We sat across from a couple we had met earlier at Waterford and had a good time talking with them. Joe ordered a bowl of Rueben Chowder, which he said was very good. We both had fish and chips and a beer and enjoyed those ole' Irish tunes playing on the jukebox. Ya gotta love those happy tunes!

To walk off some of our dinner, we did some window shopping, peeking in antique shops before making our way back to the boat. We had a fun day together.

Wednesday, June 11, 2003

We were up and ready to leave Waterford, New York, this morning when the locks opened at 7:00 a.m. The Erie Canal has a minimum depth of 12 feet from Troy to Buffalo. It traverses 35 locks as it rises, then falls, and finally rises from sea level at Troy to 565 feet above sea level at the Niagara River. Over 200 highways and railroad bridges cross the canal. The Erie Canal runs west from mile 0 here at Waterford to mile 340 at Tonawanda, New York. The first section of the Erie Canal runs from Waterford to Three Rivers where the Oswego Canal departs north. This is where you have to decide whether you will go all the way across the Erie Canal or go north towards Canada. We are going across the Erie Canal.

We started our adventure going west on the Mohawk River, which was dug out to make the Erie Canal in 1817. The Canal, which is 363 miles long, connects the Hudson River with Lake Erie and the Great Lakes. It opened up shipping from the East Coast and Europe.

Here at Waterford there is a series of five locks where boats are either lifted or lowered according to which way you are traveling. The locks here lift boats the greatest height in the shortest distance than does any other canal in the world.

Boaters may not stop overnight between these locks; therefore, they must give themselves enough time to get through all five before stopping for the day. It was 7:15 when we entered the first lock with two other boats. In locks #2 through 6 we would be lifted 151 feet above sea level.

The locks at Waterford were being upgraded because they are over 100 years old.

We had to get our lock pass at lock #3. The charge for each boat is made according to its length and by the length of time you would like to cruise on the Erie Canal. This could be a few days or all summer— it's your choice. It takes about 7-10 days to get to the other end for those on a time schedule. This schedule would make it necessary to move every day at a good speed and with no setbacks.

Before entering a lock, you should have your fenders over the side of your boat, the more the better. The lockmaster will tell you which side he wants you on before opening the huge doors to the locks. You slowly enter the lock, get your boat over to the wall, and then secure your boat with a rope hanging from the top of the cement wall of the lock. It is a good idea to have some old gloves to handle the rope because it is as wet, dirty, and slimy as the sides of the lock walls. Then you must put your own rope loosely around a cable or floating bollard located on the dock wall; the other end goes around a cleat on your boat. This holds the boat close to the wall when the water starts to rise. This is called locking up.

When the water first comes in, it creates a wave of water. The strong force first pushes you against the wall and then pushes you away from the wall. This causes you to swing around in the water, much the same as when you are being lowered, or locked down; however, it is smoother because the water is already in the lock. Your vessel swings a lot more when locking up. After this action subsides, you can enjoy the lift. This must all be done rather quickly, but after a few times you begin to get the hang of it. You must be set before the water starts coming in; it could become a very dangerous situation if you should lose control of the boat.

It's quite an experience going through a lock; in fact, the first one can be very intimidating. It doesn't take long to discover which muscles you haven't used in a while.

Then the big doors open at the other end of the lock, and the lockmaster blows a horn to signal you to let go of the ropes and proceed through them slowly. Usually the lockmaster will ask how far you are going that day and will call ahead to inform the next lockmaster you are coming through. They know how long it will take, and they will be waiting for you to help you get through the next lock faster. Most of the lockmasters are very friendly.

At lock #3 we had to decide how long we thought it would take us to get all the way through the Erie Canal. We decided it would take 10 days, and the pass cost $37.50. Every lock tender asked to see our pass and wrote down our boat registration number and boat name.

There has been so much rain this spring that waterfalls are coming off the hillsides and the canal is deeper than usual. Last winter there was a bad ice storm, which took down many trees. Crews from the Army Corps of Engineers were out with barges and chainsaws cleaning up the canal. Some of the tree damage was extensive. They have a lot of work to do to get it looking normal, but it's still very serene and pretty through here.

There are lovely old homes built from local sandstone or rock standing on the hillsides. With all the rain they have had, the lawns will be green down to the riverbanks.

It rained off and on all day with very little sunshine. I got to wear my yellow rain suit (yellow really is not my color).

We were raised 27 feet when we went through lock #7. At this point we were just four miles from Schenectady, New York. It was here that we saw a large crane sitting on the side of a rock looking for its dinner.

Going under old train track bridges with trains going over our heads was a little scary. At 1:15 p.m. we reached lock #8, where we were raised 14 feet. They were letting tons of water out over the dam because of all the rain.

We got to locks #9 and #10, where we were 255 feet above sea level. It was 5:00 and we were in Amsterdam, New York, birthplace of actor Kirk Douglas. We stopped for the night because it was getting so foggy that we couldn't see the markers. We tied up to the wall at lock #11, along with another couple, Don and Mary, who were in a 37-foot Nordic Tug (nice boat). After 37 years of marriage they have decided to do the loop. I hope they make 38!

We had dinner at 6:12 p.m., and Joe changed the oil in the engine. The sun peeked through the clouds for the first time today.

We traveled 38.2 miles today.

Thursday, June 12, 2003

We untied at 7:30 a.m. after having breakfast. We noticed more boats had come in overnight because of the weather. We let everyone go ahead of us because we go at a slower speed.

At lock #12 we were lifted 11 feet. The lockmaster here was a jolly, chubby fellow who was pleasant to have around this early in the morning. Some of the locks have a visitor's center where people can watch you lock through. Observers waved to us and we waved back; they seemed to be enjoying watching boats move through the locks. Our sailboat seemed to get a lot of attention; perhaps it is the way the pilothouse is made and the absence of a mast that attracts attention. She looks like a riverboat.

After getting through the lock, we went up the canal through Fonda, New York, where the Henry Fonda clan is from. We could see the Adirondack Mountain range off in the distance. The mountains reach up to the sky and are actually in the clouds. Cruising along, we saw lots of ducks with ducklings trailing behind them in the water. Mother Nature is wonderful!

Wild yellow irises grew all along the riverbank for miles; purple and white wild phlox covered the banks also. I would love to have gotten a start of the irises, but it was too dangerous to get that close to the bank. I thought Joe could swim over, but he wasn't interested in doing so. He reminded me we didn't have a way to keep them alive, to which I replied that we were surrounded by water that could be used for that purpose. Nevertheless, I still didn't get any flowers. It was a very pretty scene through here.

A big boat passed us going 15 mph, and the speed limit on the canal is 10 mph. This caused us to get over in the shallow water close to the bank, almost grounding us. A wave of water hitting a boat can toss it back and forth, and these big waves cause soil erosion along the banks. This is the reason speed limits are imposed; but, as on highways, not everyone obeys them. The people who own those big boats don't seem to be very considerate of other boaters. It seems that kind of people are everywhere—on land and in the water.

We arrived at lock #17, which is impressive. Not only is it the highest lift lock on the Erie Canal, it is one of only two locks in North America where the entrance gate is lifted above the boater. All of the other locks open like a gate, letting the water come in slowly through the opening. This one opens like a garage door, and the water comes in under it like a flood. This is a tremendous amount of cement and steel to be raised over the boat.

We were lifted up 40 feet; that is a lot of water. With the gate going over the top of the boat, we knew we were going to get wet. Luckily, we could stay under our bimini until we got over to the wall. That certainly was quite an experience. Four other boats locked through with us.

Just past the lock is Herkimer, New York, where the Erie Canal leaves the Mohawk River and becomes a true canal. It runs alongside the narrow winding river as it approaches the high point of the eastern section. We could see the old original trail alongside the canal where mules once pulled the canal boats through and where the old locks used to be. This was a true learning experience about the canal's history. We could actually see the trail as we went along. If only I had the video camera to capture all this.

Lock #18 raised us up another twenty feet; we were 383 feet above sea level.

Traveling on up the canal, we stopped for the night just above lock #19 in Ilion, New York, and tied up at the wall at 6:15 p.m. We had the spot all to ourselves, making for a nice, quiet night.

We traveled 56 miles today.

Friday, June 13, 2003

Up this morning at 7:15, we saw that the day was cloudy with a misty rain. We headed across the canal to lock #20, which will take us up another 21 feet. More flowers were growing along the bank, and in front of us we saw a deer swimming across the canal.

We passed a place where the canal is dammed up; the dam is at the spot where creeks used to branch off. Fallen trees and logs were trapped there. We passed under more bridges that spanned the canal. Deer grazed on the banks and paid no attention to us. An advantage of going slowly is that we can really enjoy the wildlife and natural beauty; we would miss all this if we were in a fast boat. This is so enjoyable, and I am glad I came along on the trip.

We were at the highest level of the east section of the canal at 420 feet as we headed to lock #21. We were going through Rome, New York, where the middle section of the Erie Canal starts.

Going west, this is where the canal's elevation first drops as it approaches the level of the Oswego River. Those heading to Canada would turn here. The Erie Canal then rises in elevation as it follows the Seneca River westward and slowly rises to the elevation of the Cayuga-Seneca Canal. It continues to rise at the locks in Lyons, New York.

This section of the canal has many attractions. I always wanted to go to Rome, but we didn't stop there because it looked like rain. We still had some daylight left and we wanted to get farther up the canal.

Lock #21 was the first lock where we locked down 25 feet. After locks #22 and #23, we had locked down a total of 57 feet to a level of 363 feet above sea level.

We stopped at 1:12 p.m. at Sylvan Beach because the rain and fog were making it difficult to see the navigational markers. Sylvan Beach is east of Oneida Lake, the largest body of water on the Erie Canal.

Oneida Lake is 20 miles long and three miles wide. It should be crossed only after careful consideration of the weather. It is very clean, and often you can see eight to ten feet down in the water. This means it is shallow and can be dangerous if the wind should pick up.

After securing the boat to the dock, Joe put the last two cans of fuel we have on board into the fuel tank. When we get across the lake, we will be looking for fuel.

This looks like a good place to stop in bad weather. In case we have to stay a few days, we will have good restaurants and the town is within walking distance. There is even a small amusement park here—lots of things to see and do.

The rain let up, and we went to do the laundry. By the time we finished, rain was falling again. We waited for a break in the rain and made a dash for Eddie's, a family diner across the street. It was time for dinner and we were hungry. We were cold and damp, and the hot soup on the menu hit the spot, along with a delicious hot meal. While waiting for the rain to stop, we enjoyed a refill of iced tea and talked with the waitress.

As soon as the rain let up, we hurried out with the laundry in plastic bags on a two-wheel cart, which Joe was dragging through mud puddles. Luckily, only the socks got wet; I rinsed them off and hung them everywhere I could. We ended up taking them back to the Laundromat to dry them. We had to laugh or we would have cried; I'm so tired of the rain.

It has been raining so long that we are leaving all the clothes in the plastic bags to keep them dry. But the sun will shine again and all will be dry once more in the world of boating! I hope!

The rain stopped at 8:30 p.m. Let's hope we will have sunshine now for a few days. We really could use some warm air to dry out everything and everyone. I think my toes are beginning to web! Ha!

We traveled 34.1 miles today.

Saturday, June 14, 2003

It's 8:00 a.m. and we're still at Sylvan Beach, New York, because it was too foggy to go across the lake.

We walked to town for breakfast at Labella's Pancake House, which we saw yesterday when we went to the laundromat. Autographed pictures of stars covered the walls. In the midst of this atmosphere, we ordered silver dollar pancakes. After eating these yummy pancakes, we understood why they are famous for their pancakes. With full tummies, we walked over the bridge to Verona, New York, to a marina; we wanted to stretch our legs and check out the boats.

Rain started falling again as we walked back to the boat, making us walk a little faster. At 5:00 it stopped again, permitting us to walk over to" Yesterday's" Royal Restaurant at the marina. It looks like an old-fashioned eatery, and they serve good old-fashioned ice cream, something we don't get much of on the boat. Joe loves vanilla ice cream. After our meal, I took a walk around the park; Joe went back to the boat to make coffee for morning.

After it quit raining again, a lot of people strolled along the boardwalk. Children enjoyed their ice cream cones and their parents enjoyed the fresh air. This was the first nice day they have had in a while to get out for fresh air and to look at boats.

As I came back up the boardwalk, I noticed two young girls with a camera standing in front of "Whoosher" taking pictures of each other. When I approached the boat, they said, "Oh, is this your boat? We just love it." They explained they were pretending that it was their boat and were taking pictures to show their friends back home. They didn't know anyone was on board; of course, Joe didn't even have a clue the girls were out there. I told them they could take all the pictures they wanted. How funny is that?

With all the big fancy boats here, they chose to take a picture of "Whoosher." She does get a lot of attention everywhere we go. She is not your average looking sailboat. With the big windows on the pilothouse and no mast, she looks like a little riverboat.

Looking out, we noticed everyone heading to the other end of the boardwalk; we had to go see what was going on. When we got there, we found out that earlier today the wind and waves had forced two fishermen up against the rocks at the breakwater and had trapped them. The police rescue boat couldn't get in close enough to help because the wind kept the water too choppy and dangerous even for the rescue boats. This was not a good situation.

People in kayaks were trying to get in closer, but they were not having any luck, either. Finally, the fishermen walked across the rocks, leaving their boat. They were soaking wet and a little shook up, but they were lucky they didn't drown. Those diehard fishermen will go down with their boats, or at least first make sure nothing will happen to it.

As we walked back, we stopped to talk with a couple, Larry and Sue, who were on a trawler named "Lanoka." They were making the loop with their Brittany spaniel. Maybe we will meet them again somewhere on the canal.

After getting back to the boat, we noticed two Carroll Shelby Cobra cars parked at the Crazy Crab restaurant right in front of our boat. They were classic originals in mint condition and were drawing a lot of attention from people on the boardwalk. We had to get pictures of them for Gregg (Joe's brother-in-law), who is a car buff.

We are hoping for a nice dry day tomorrow.

Sunday, June 15, 2003 (Father's Day)

It looked like it was going to be a beautiful Father's Day. It was a bit foggy, but it seemed to be burning off fast. We left Sylvan Beach at 7:20 a.m. and started across Oneida Lake. The forecast called for 10-15 mph winds. We made it across the lake with no problems; it turned out to be a beautiful day to cross it.

We looked for a marina to fuel up, and at 12:00 p.m. we pulled into the Ess-Kay Yard, Inc. The lady marina owner came out to welcome us. We got our fuel and a pump-out, and Larry and Sue on "Lonaka" pulled up. We exchanged names for future reference. They weren't yet sure which way they were going on the loop, maybe through Oswego.

Joe told the marina owner about wanting to stop somewhere around Toledo, Ohio, to leave our boat for a few weeks to go back to Indiana. She told us about a marina in Sandusky, just before getting to Toledo, which is owned by some very nice people she knew personally. She gave us the name of the owner and the phone number of Battery Park Marina at Sandusky. She said to tell them how we had gotten their name and number and that they would work with us. She is another nice person we have met on this trip.

As we continued across the canal, we noticed the homes built on the high banks along here. Ladders reached down the bank to the canal or the docks in front of many of these homes. As we went through the small towns, we saw many people fishing. It would seem that they depend on the water for their supper at times, and perhaps for their survival.

We had a good day on the water. We could smell the BBQ's of those taking advantage of the nice weather we are finally getting on land and water. It's great to have this wonderful weather again.

At lock #23 we were lifted seven feet. There was another visitor's center there where people could sit and watch you lock through. We just smiled and waved back to them. Their friendliness sort of makes your day!

We passed the point where you can go up the Oswego River toward Canada, but we stayed on course for Lake Erie. I was out on the bow looking for the signs that direct you to the right canal.

Captain Joe at the wheel

If we missed them, we could be heading for Canada and not even know it for miles.

More geese and flowers appeared along this stretch of the canal. We both love the yellow irises that brighten the banks. We were in the Seneca River past Lake Ononadga. The canal twisted and turned, making it necessary to pay close attention to the maps and charts. It all began to look the same along the riverbanks. Thank goodness, there were mile markers located on trees or on a post so that we could match up with the charts. Sometimes they were hard to find; but, like puzzle pieces, they can be found if you keep looking.

It was so peaceful through there. We were sitting out in the cockpit, going along at six knots, when all of a sudden it occurred to us that we might not be on the right canal. We checked the compass, and we were okay.

At lock #24 at Baldwinville we locked up 11 feet. We almost missed our turn at Cross Lake, but we figured it out just in time to stay on the Erie Canal. There were four canals going off in four different directions. You can't let down your guard for one minute through here.

We stopped at 5:45 p.m. along the wall outside an abandoned restaurant called Smitty's Roadside Tavern. There was a picnic table in a little clearing at the side of the wall, and another boat was tied up here. The captain came over to help us tie up to the wall. This wall was a bit too tall for me to reach the cleats with our ropes, so it was nice to have the help.

Joe talked with him and found out that he had built his boat himself. He lived around the area and was out enjoying the canal for a few days. Joe would love to build his own boat to live on.

We were relaxing on the boat after dinner when a young couple walked out to the wall to fish. Watching the young man and his girl friend was entertaining enough; but when he finally caught a fish, reeled it in, held it up, looked over at Joe and me sitting in our boat, and asked us if he could keep it, we burst out laughing. We told him it was okay with us if he kept the fish. Then he wanted to know what kind of fish it was. Joe showed him how to hold a catfish and explained how to clean it. The young man, who appeared to be about 18, was so excited to have caught his first fish. He told us he was going to take it home, cook it, and eat it.

We didn't see him catch any more fish. We thought that he and his girl friend had other plans for the evening, so we just turned in for the night. Boating is exhausting work. By the time you get dinner and everything is cleaned up, you are ready to hit the sack!

We traveled 60.3 miles today.

Monday, June 16, 2003

We got up, had our coffee, and went out to the picnic table where I gave Joe a much-needed haircut. We got away about 9:20 a.m.

Except for a couple of fishermen in jon boats, we had the canal all to ourselves. It was a beautiful sunny morning with a wonderful scent in the air. Cruising along this calm, quiet canal today was very enjoyable. We can understand how you could spend a whole summer just cruising up and down the Erie Canal.

Today we saw our first turtle since leaving the rivers in Carolina.

We reached several locks today: lock #25, a lift of six feet; lock #26, another lift of six feet; lock #27, a lift of 12 feet; lock #28A, a lift of 20 feet; and lock #28B, a lift of 12 feet. We are now 398 feet above sea level.

We stopped in Newark, New York, at 4:00 p.m. The welcome center was closed for the night, but a couple already docked for the night came over and told us they would share the key to the shower room with us. This was very kind and much appreciated; we were ready for a refreshing shower. In talking with the couple, we found out that they were starting the loop from Newark and were doing it backwards.

The facilities here were all new with free washer and dryer; this was a first on the trip. Usually the amount charged for doing laundry is similar to that charged by a laundromat.

Right behind us there is an old railroad bridge on which the four corners of an American flag are attached to its side. What a wonderful sight!

We walked to town and ate at the Corner Grill. Joe and I both had the southwestern chicken salad, an excellent choice.

The streets are rolled up early here, so we walked back to the boat to settle in for the night. I love stopping in these small towns, walking through them, and seeing the different homes and the town's layout. These small towns are so accommodating to boaters. This has been a good day on the water.

We traveled 37.8 miles today.

Tuesday, June 17, 2003

Starting at 7:00 a.m. on another beautiful sunny day, we had gone under two bridges by 7:05. This morning we saw a squirrel swimming across the canal. To make sure we were seeing correctly, we pulled up beside it. I took its picture, but it was in the shadow of the boat and didn't show up. The canal started getting narrow; lots of fallen trees in the waterway made it difficult to get through in places.

At Macedon, New York, we reached lock #29, locking up 16 feet, and lock #30, locking another 16 feet.

We saw a well-traveled bicycle path along the canal here. We have already seen several bicyclists today. Lots of people waved as we went by; they seem to be a little friendlier in western New York.

Fairport is the starting point of the western section of the canal. It most closely resembles the original Erie Canal with a ditch dug through the landscape and a towpath on both sides.

While traveling through Fairport, New York, we encountered a big tour boat loaded with school children on a field trip. The lock tender told us the schools do this every year at this time; the children learn about the Erie Canal and the locks. How lucky are they?

Because the tour boat had priority in the canal, we had to drop in behind it. We got ready to go through lock #32, a 25-foot lock up, and then right into lock #33, another 25-foot lock up. We were 512 feet above sea level at that point.

We went under some more lift bridges. The lift bridges on the Erie Canal are different from those on the Inter Coastal Waterway. They offer clearance of about 17 feet when open. The Erie Canal is the main reason we left our mast (a 42-foot pole) back in Fort Myers. It would have had to be unstepped (taken down) back at Troy before entering the canal. It also would have been something else for Joe to hit his head on.

Roving operators operate most of the bridges. You might have to wait for an operator to get to the second or third bridge; bridges are usually around three miles apart. Most of the bridges and the lift bridges on the Erie Canal have the same clearance. It is worth the wait, however, because the travel through here has been a wonderful experience so far.

Five miles past the lock is a four-mile-long section of the canal, often referred to as the Rock Cut. This required some of the most extensive excavation of the entire canal. The deep cut was made through solid rock by pioneers, and we can only imagine how hard it must have been to do this without the modern earth moving equipment we have today. I loved the rocks through here.

The homes and roads through here are closer to the canal. The homes are lower than the canal bank, and we could see only the rooftops of the home—a strange sight! We stopped at the Park Avenue Bridge at Brockport, New York, at 4:10 p.m.

We walked a mile to a Wal-Mart (mostly uphill) and ate at a Chinese Buffet, again eating too much. Thank God, the walk back was mostly downhill because we were loaded down with Wal-Mart bags. We really were in need of supplies. We were glad to get back to the boat; the bags were getting heavy.

We traveled 52.5 miles today.

Wednesday, June 18, 2003

We were under way this morning at 8:10 a.m.; the weather was windy with not much sun. We went under the Brockport Main Street Bridge. Making it to Albion and then on up to Knowlesville, we were at the place where the canal crosses over the Calvert Road aqueduct, the only place the Erie Canal can be driven under. Then five miles farther down, the Erie Canal crosses over the Orchard Creek aqueduct, so there is water going under water. How fascinating is that?

Just going through that stretch, we went under 12 lift bridges and two locks, plus dozens of regular bridges.

The trip through Medina, New York, is beautiful. Most of the buildings in this old town are built with sandstone from local quarries that have been in operation more than 80 years. The quarries have even exported their sandstone to both Cuba and England. The buildings and homes are still in very good condition after all these years.

A replica of Noah's ark appeared in one of the backyards. I thought it was a very clever and appropriate display to be seen by those going down the canal.

Reaching Lockport, we went through locks #34 and #35 and were locked up 50 feet. At this point, we were 564 feet above sea level. It was difficult to imagine we had been going uphill all this time while in the water system. There is no stopping between these two locks. When coming out of #34, you go right into #35; this was quite an experience. There was room for one boat to tie up behind the north lock wall, and the lockmaster said we could tie up there. It was an easy walk to town and it was free for the night.

An overflow right beside these locks looks like a giant waterfall. It is where the original five locks used to be years ago.

It was 4:15 when we stopped. Shortly afterward, we walked to town to drop off film at a Walgreen Pharmacy and strolled around town looking at the old historic homes built from local sandstone. Their green lawns and big urns stuffed with flowers created a photo opportunity.

We ate at Friendly's, a restaurant that catered to families with children. Not only was it colorfully attractive to children, it included ice cream of all flavors with the meals. We had their New England fish and chips with a cold Coca Cola. Our tummies must be shrinking (which is good) because we didn't have room for any ice cream (hard to believe). Could it be that we simply stuffed ourselves so much that there was no room for ice cream?

We walked over the largest and widest bridge on the Erie Canal, which is located here in Lockport, picked up the developed pictures, and then returned to our boat. Joe made coffee for morning, and we relaxed a while before going to bed. This was a good day.

We traveled 42 miles today.

Thursday, June 19, 2003

At 9:30 we were leaving the dock a bit later than usual. There were a few sprinkles on the windshield. As we motored down the canal, we went past more rock walls on both sides. Dozens and dozens of Canada geese and ducks were everywhere. I think the Canada geese have forgotten how to get back to Canada.

We went through Pendleton, New York at 12:45. We used to live in Pendleton, Indiana, and we've been through Pendleton, Texas. I wonder how many more Pendleton's there are.

We stopped at Tonawanda, New York, which is the stopping point before crossing Lake Erie. We will have to wait here for the wind to change to the south so we can cross the lake; it looks like that may be Monday.

Here at Tonawanda, we are tied to a brand new wall along the Delaware Street Bridge. This is in the middle of town with restaurants and stores all within walking distance. Tonawanda is on one side of the bridge, North Tonawanda is on the other side, and the Erie Canal goes right down the middle. It is very pretty here.

Here is "Whoosher" second boat back.

Staying on the boat, we relaxed, took showers, and fixed dinner onboard. Joe helped tie up a sailboat that came in. The captain told Joe he is going around the world all by himself. Joe wished him good luck and took our map of the Hudson River to him. This man didn't even have any maps. (Not very smart)

The dock master here told us he works at the basketball camps at Indiana University in Bloomington, Indiana, during the summer. He has come to the boat to talk basketball with Joe; he is a nice young man.

The wall along here has shade trees with benches under them; there is a wide sidewalk that accommodates bicycles. The restrooms and showers are very nice and clean.

All across the Erie Canal we have found that the towns are boat friendly with walls you can easily tie up to, and there are stores and restaurants within walking distance. The docks, most of the time, are free or are very reasonably priced. Most docks have both water and electric hookups. Crossing the Erie Canal has been an enjoyable experience. My wish is that everyone has the chance to have this experience in his lifetime. And to think that I almost didn't make it myself!

We traveled 21 miles today.

Friday, June 20, 2003

After getting to sleep in for a change, we had our coffee and then walked over to McDonald's for breakfast. Our plans for today included taking a bus to Niagara Falls. Joe has decided to combine this trip with a honeymoon and take me to see the falls. How sweet is that?

We finally figured out the bus schedule with the help of some nice folks who ride it every day. As the time drew near for us to get off the bus, the driver, guessing we were tourists, asked us where we were going. When it was time to change buses, he told us to stay on his bus and he would take us closer to the falls. In fact, he took us within six blocks of the falls, pointed us in the right direction, and told us when to be back at the bus stop. He was very kind to us; we couldn't have asked for anyone better.

He didn't want a tip, but we tipped him anyway. He had gone out of his way to help us, and we appreciated it.

We walked just a few blocks to Niagara Falls Park, went through the botanical gardens, and then crossed the Niagara River Bridge. From the bridge we could see the water flowing over huge rocks before going over the falls. We heard the falls as soon as we were in the park and saw the mist in the air. As we got closer, we could feel the mist on our faces. At the falls the sound of the water is deafening, but the view is spectacular and breathtaking. Words cannot describe it.

Looking down over a ledge, we saw the "Maid of the Mist," the tour boat that goes within a few feet of the waterfall. It was scary looking down from the top, but we could see how close the boat went to the falls. The undertow current looked strong enough to sink the boat in a second. Passengers on the boat wear rain gear to protect themselves from getting wet as they sail near the falls. The "Maid of the Mist" is a fairly large tour boat, but from the ledge it looked like a little toy.

I took lots of pictures. The view from the ledge was so beautiful. I just stood there looking out over the falls trying to take it all in. Standing on the American side looking over to the Canadian side presented a spectacular view. The whole experience was simply hypnotizing.

As we walked across Goat Island and then back across the park, we stopped to buy a T-shirt with "Honeymoon City" on it and some postcards to send to the kids.

On our way back to the bus station, I wanted to find the Hard Rock Café. I had seen it as we came in on the bus, but we couldn't find it. Afraid of missing the bus, we headed back to the station. We timed it perfectly because the bus pulled in shortly after we got there. We were on our way back to Tonawanda. Whew!

We had a perfectly wonderful day together at the falls. I wish we could have had dinner in Niagara Falls, but the bus schedule was not cooperative.

When we got back to town, we discovered they were having Canal Days this weekend in Tonawanda. There would be bands and food stands. We could hear the band walking over to get something to eat.

It was playing Buddy Holly tunes, oldies but goodies, which bring back some good memories.

Getting back to the boat and relaxing out in the cockpit, we listened to the band playing "Peggy Sue" and "Wake up, Little Susie." I wanted to get up and dance. Darn—no dance floor!

What a good day we had!

Saturday, June 21, 2003

We were up and off to McDonald's again this morning. Today we went the opposite direction to Buffalo, New York, by bus. We need a chip for the GPS in order to cross Lake Erie, so we were on our way to find a West Marine store. This involved a different bus schedule and bus driver. Also, it was raining, and I was in my yellow rain suit.

After arriving in Buffalo, we had to change buses to get to the marine store. The lady bus driver was a little "dingy," but nice. She said she would be back at the corner where we got off in one hour. If we would walk the seven blocks to the store and come back to this corner, she would watch for us and take us back to transfer to the bus back to town. I told her I should be easy to spot—I would be the one in a yellow suit!

We hustled to get the chip and returned to the corner. Here she came, right on time. We had a half hour wait after getting back to the bus stop, so we had lunch at the Subway on the corner.

We were back in Tonawanda just in time to watch the parade. The streets were blocked off, and the bus driver couldn't get to the bus stop. He had to circle the block, putting everyone on the bus in a panic. We got off just around the corner from our boat, which worked out well for us. Fortunately, the rain had stopped just in time for the parade, and we stood on the corner watching it before heading back to the boat for supper.

The concert tonight was across the bridge in North Tonawanda. We walked over to the concert area, finding an antique store on our way. We love walking through antique shops just to look around. Joe is always looking for turkeys and I'm always just looking! You never know what treasure you will find.

The rock-n-roll band that played tonight drew a large crowd. This is not really our favorite kind of music, so we headed back to the boat to enjoy the evening just sitting, relaxing, and watching the boats and the people. Lots of boats have come in for the festival.

Sunday, June 22, 2003

We woke up to a beautiful day; the sun came out and it warmed up. This was a good day just to kick back and enjoy the surroundings.

We have had a parade of boats back and forth on the canal all day from 9:30 a.m. until 7:30 p.m. It's amazing how many of them have dogs on board, all shapes and sizes.

Everyone must be in town for the festival. There are so many boats that they are rafting four boats deep, leaving just enough room to get down the center of the canal. They are jammed in here like sardines. I hope no one has to leave in a hurry.

Joe worked on the boat while I washed down the front cabin and the galley. After all the rain, mildew had taken over because of the dampness. Now the walls are white and the boat smells fresh again. Nice!

I walked to the grocery store for supplies, passing the antique store we saw yesterday. I went in to get the turquoise blue heart-shaped necklace I had found there.

I fixed supper on the boat, and we sat out in the cockpit watching the parade of boats. We were having a very enjoyable evening when the Tonawanda marina police patrol came over to our boat to ask if we knew that we were missing a letter in the vessel registration number on the right front bow.

Of course, we didn't know it or we would have gotten one yesterday in Buffalo. We told him we were not aware of this; we had come all the way from Florida through the canal and about 35 locks. The lockmasters had taken our registration number, and no one had said a word to us about it. We told him we would replace it as soon as possible. He took Joe's driver's license and the boat registration and left in his boat for half an hour. Finally, he came back and gave us a ticket for not having a valid registration sticker on the starboard (right) side of our vessel; he didn't even bother to check the left side for a registration sticker.

This man didn't know his index finger from his thumb. We were issued one sticker to be put on the port (left) side, which we had if he had only checked, but he would have had to get out of his boat. He was a real jerk!

Joe was so mad I thought he was going to have a stroke, and I was so mad I couldn't even talk. We were registered correctly, and this was going to be on Joe's driving record, hanging over his head the rest of the trip. Also, the ticket had a court appearance date on it to appear in court here in two weeks. We couldn't stay here two more weeks; we were planning to leave tomorrow morning. Joe said we would write a letter to the judge explaining all this. I called the registration office at the courthouse in Florida to check with them. I was told that we were registered correctly in the computer, and all the patrol had to do was check it. We were probably safe, but it still was very upsetting. We were having such a nice day, and this ruined our whole stay here. The dock master came by; he couldn't believe it either. He said he had never heard of anyone getting a ticket for that in all the time he had worked here.

We had our showers and got everything ready to take off in the morning. The weather for the next few days looks good for starting across Lake Erie. We are going!

CHAPTER 3
GREAT LAKES
TONAWANDA , N.Y.- - - CHICAGO, ILLIN

Monday, June 23, 2003

We left Tonawanda at 7:15 a.m. with a beautiful day coming up. As we went up the canal, we had to make sure we turned left on the Niagara River. A right turn would take us to Niagara Falls.

We headed to the Black Rock lock, the last one on the canal; it is also a federal lock. We went up only five feet and were level with Lake Erie. We called the lockmaster, who told us to enter and float around in the middle since we were the only ones going through. Not having to hold on to a rope as we went through the lock was a different experience; we got through this one with no problem. Lake Erie, here we come!

This is a big body of water. At first we had 1-2 foot seas; but as we went farther, a west wind calmed the water and it turned out to be a good day. We were headed southwest. We anchored at Dunkirk, New York, at 4:15 p.m. behind a breakwater. A breakwater is a structure built to protect a harbor or beach from the force of waves coming in from a big body of water.

We had a most vivid sunset on the lake with colors of oranges and blues across the sky. It was a gorgeous watercolor picture. We had a beautiful day on Lake Erie!

We traveled 50.8 miles today.

Tuesday, June 24, 2003

Another beautiful day, sunshine, a smiling husband, eggs and grits for breakfast, and coffee all made for a good start for the day. We pulled anchor at 7:30 a.m.

Lake Erie was calm and a very pretty blue-green color as we headed for Erie, Pennsylvania, with very little wind. The good news is that Joe got the autopilot working just in time to cross the lake. I think he stopped and read the directions. He named it Popeye. It will be a big help in crossing the lakes (I hope).

We could see the Allegheny Mountains off to the southeast. We had planned to stop at Erie, but it was only 2:00 when we got there, which was too early to stop. Because we were making good time on smooth water and the autopilot was doing a great job of steering, we decided to take advantage of the good weather and cross the lake before bad weather came in. This can happen in a heartbeat on the water.

Joe enjoyed sitting with me at the table in the galley and helping me watch for logs and boats while Popeye did the steering. So far, he's doing a good job and giving the captain a rest.

So that we could keep going, I fixed dinner while we were under way; I even made coffee. We knew it would be almost dark when we finally anchored for the night. Sorry, Rodger, we sort of pushed it today.

Lake Erie can turn on you at any time, and we wanted to get across while the weather was still good. We anchored in a harbor outside Ashtabula, Ohio, at 8:00 p.m. Having gotten everything done early, we had dinner by candlelight so we wouldn't run down the batteries while anchored.

We put in the last two cans of fuel and changed the oil and filter (every 70 miles). We can go for days on a tank of fuel, which is a nice thing about this diesel engine.

We noticed there are not any birds on the water. I was curious about this and wondered if it was because of a lack of something to feed on because of pollution in the water. This is not a good sign. We had a great day on the water today.

We traveled 85.6 miles today.

Wednesday, June 25, 2003

At 6:30 a.m. Joe was pulling the anchor. As we were leaving the Ashtabula anchorage, I took a picture of an impressive old building located at the entrance to the harbor. I would guess that it probably was once a lighthouse years ago.

We had a 10-15 mph wind from the southwest as we headed for Lorain, Ohio. There was nothing but water any direction we looked. Thanks to the autopilot, we made good time.

The marine weather information gave a prediction of foul weather coming in by the end of the week, so we will try to get to Sandusky, Ohio, before it gets here. At 6:15 p.m. we pulled into our anchorage at Lorain. We made good mileage today using Popeye; I'm sure Joe's happy he got it working in time to be of help. This takes a lot of the work out of steering across big bodies of water. The course can be programmed; it's great if the water is not too rough.

We saw kids on their Ski-Do's and small sailboats out enjoying the water back in the cove. Ski-Do's can make waves and mess up a calm anchorage. Their waves rock the boat and make it difficult to get anything done inside. Hopefully, it settles down when the sun sets, and it looks like another beautiful sunset on the water tonight.

We traveled 79.7 miles today.

Thursday, June 26, 2003

Pulling anchor at 6:30 a.m. leaving Lorain, Ohio headed for Sandusky, Ohio. We started out cutting across a 24 mile cove to save time, but the wind picked up making it too rough on the beam. We went toward shore to get into calmer waters. The extra distance was worth having calmer water. There was a storm coming in and we wanted to get to the safe harbor at Sandusky before it hit.

We arrived at Battery Park Marina in Sandusky, Ohio, at 11:30 a.m. just as the storm arrived with wind and rain making it a rough entrance into the marina. I was glad to get into the marina behind the breakwater.

The lady at Ess-Kay Marina outside Sylvan Beach had told us about this place. It seems to be a nice marina and well maintained. We will leave the boat here for a few weeks to go home to Shoals, Indiana, to celebrate the Fourth of July with our kids and friends.

We had planned to rent a car to drive home, but there's no car rental close to us. So, we called our son's to come get us.

They told us it was no problem and that they would leave first thing in the morning. This means they should arrive just in time for dinner. There is a Damon's restaurant near the marina office; we can treat the boys and then take off for home. I can't wait to see everyone; I really miss them.

We have gone 2,397 miles thus far on our journey. It will feel so good to sleep on a real bed for a few weeks.

We traveled 34.1 miles today.

Wednesday, July 16, 2003

We are back on the boat after three wonderful weeks at home getting to see all our friends and family. The boys brought us back to Sandusky, Ohio.

We stopped for supplies before going into the marina, taking advantage of a vehicle and two strong boys to help us carry everything to the boat. We hated to see the boys leave, but they needed to get back home before it got late.

In getting settled on the boat, we found it had been engulfed with spiders during our absence. I don't like spiders, and Joe spent the evening on deck killing them as fast as he could find them. I kept him busy by pointing out all the spiders I could see from the safety of the boat's interior. Thank God, they were all outside, or I would have been sleeping on a park bench.

The tall ships were scheduled to come into the harbor today and be on display over the weekend. We stayed on board getting the boat back in shape, watching for them to enter the harbor. Hearing a loud explosion and wondering what was going on, I looked out to see everyone hurrying to the breakwater and I knew they were coming in. The big tall masts and sails came into view, and I ran to the end of the dock to take pictures of the ships. Seeing a tall ship come into a harbor under sail is an awesome sight.

One of the ships, named "Windy" from Chicago, had cannons on board. The cannons are fired when the ship enters a harbor; this certainly gets your attention. I thought we were under attack!

Most of these ships are 150 feet long, with three masts, and a crew of up to 150 people. This is a big schooner! Watching them come into a harbor is an impressive sight. An opportunity to see them should not be missed.

Thursday, July 17, 2003

Our plans for today included going to see the tall ships this afternoon and taking in the festival in uptown Sandusky. We found out that "Windy I" and "Windy II" would be on display. "Windy II" was the one firing her cannons to announce her arrival in the harbor.

We certainly lucked out by getting to see the tall ships come into port with their sails up. The tall ship "Niagara" presented a magnificent sight, along with the others docked in the harbor around the peninsula. From the dock at Battery Park Marina we could see the tall masts above the treetops. We decided to go to town tomorrow when the festival will be in full swing.

It has been a nice day, but the wind is picking up. We have decided to stay here one more day. We cleaned the boat and put things away while waiting for the weather to calm down so we can cross Lake Erie over to the Detroit River. If the weather cooperates, we will go. We are learning the weather is your worst enemy while out on the water.

Friday, July 19, 2003

We had planned to leave today, but northeast winds of 15-20 knots made it unfit to take the boat out. Instead, Joe worked on the stove, putting new packing in the handles. He changed both filters so we will be all set to leave Saturday if the winds die down.

After Joe finished his chores, we walked to town to see the tall ships and get a bite to eat. At the pier where the ships were anchored, we found a little yard barn where fish sandwiches were being served. Because of the long line of people waiting to order, we concluded that the locals knew that good food was served here. Learning that walleye and perch sandwiches were on the menu, we got in line and ordered fish sandwiches and fries. Joe ordered two sandwiches and I ordered one;

they were delicious. Joe wished he had ordered more. Our boys would have loved this, but I know they enjoyed their food at Damon's.

Next, we walked over to see the tall ships. They are manned by college students who sign up for the summer to go on a circuit tour around the country. Learning to operate them is physically challenging, and learning to do this in just one summer is quite a learning experience for the students. I know my little boat has been a learning experience, and it's like a dinghy compared to one of these ships.

It was possible to go aboard; but since we had been on one in Fort Myers, we decided to go uptown looking through antique shops. After this, we sat on a bench enjoying a dish of ice cream before going to see the antique cars that were in town for the weekend.

We thoroughly enjoyed our day in Sandusky. Back on the boat now, we are ready for the weather to improve so we can get on with the "Great Circle."

Saturday, July 19. 2003

After eating breakfast, we left the dock at 7:00 a.m. to go to the fuel dock so we could be first in line when it opened at 8:00.

It looked like it would be a great day to be on the water; but, since it was a Saturday, all the weekend warriors would be heading to the Kelley and South Bass Islands. These islands, which can be reached only by boat, are just a few miles off the coast; all the locals go there on the weekends for fun. We passed the islands on our way across the west end of the lake as we headed for the Detroit River

The water was rough, going up the Detroit River causing us to do a lot of rolling. The current was strong, we were going 6 mile an hour through the water going into a 4 mile and hour current taking us down to a 2 mph over the bottom, it felt like we were barely moving. Fighting the current and wind all day was difficult for Joe.

There was no marina or any place to anchor until we got to the Erma Henderson Park Marina across from Belle Island outside Detroit, Michigan. I called ahead for a slip, and we got to the marina about 8:00 p.m. It is about three miles from Lake Saint Clair.

After settling in at the marina, we walked across the street to McDonald's. It was good to stretch the old legs and get off the boat for a while after fighting the wind and water for 12 hours. It was a long day, especially after not being on board for three weeks. We have to get our sea legs back.

We traveled 74.5 miles today.

Sunday, July 20, 2003

This morning we called our friends from Indiana, Richard and Margaret, who live here now. We were not sure how close to the marina they live, but we found out they are only about a half hour away. Margaret and her daughters, Jessica and Ashley, came to the boat to visit. It was good to see them.

When they arrived, they insisted we go back to the house for supper with them. Margaret had fixed a feast, baked ham with all the delicious trimmings. As if we weren't already sufficiently stuffed, she sent leftovers with us to enjoy tomorrow.

We had a really nice visit with them and enjoyed seeing them. We can't believe how grown up the girls have become and all the things they are doing now. They wanted us to stay over, but we had to get back to the boat. Margaret and the girls took us back around 5:00 and walked back to the boat with us. The girls wanted to come aboard to see inside it. They thought the boat was really neat, but weren't too sure about its moving around. They found it difficult to stand up and keep their balance.

They hated to leave us, but we finally said our goodbyes with hugs and promises to keep in touch with them along the way. Joe took pictures to put in our scrapbook of the trip.

After a great day visiting with our friends, we settled in for the night, stuffed like two turkeys. Joe got the coffee ready for morning, and we relaxed while thinking how lucky we are to have such nice friends. Thank you, Margaret, for a fabulous meal and for being such a good friend.

The Erma Henderson Park Marina is a very nice clean place with picnic tables and BBQ grills for your use. Some people are using the BBQ grills right now. We are still stuffed from dinner, but it smells good.

Tomorrow we will be back on The Loop.

Monday, July 21, 2003

We left Detroit at 10:15 a.m. after a rainy and windy night at the marina. Going across Lake Saint Clair was smooth.

Lake Saint Clair is a shallow, almost round, lake 24 miles in diameter. Good weather is needed for crossing it, and we had a good crossing. We could see big black storm clouds forming up ahead. We called ahead to the South Channel Yacht Club (SCYC) just off the St. Clair River and pulled in there at 2:15. At 4:15 the clouds cut loose, and we had a good lightning storm.

The marina here, while not fancy, is a good safe harbor in a storm. We got here just in time; more boats started pulling in as the rain came down in buckets. Luckily, the worst part of the storm missed us, but rain and thunderstorms are predicted for all week.

We still had the good leftovers Margaret gave us; I love it when I don't have to cook.

We had a short day, going only 24.7 miles.

Tuesday, July 22, 2003

We pulled out of SCYC at 8:00 a.m. on a cloudy day. The water was calm on the Saint Clair River, but the current was strong. We could go only 2 mph; it was slow going but at least we were moving.

Four lake ships passed us, but we got out of their way and all went smoothly. A lot of freight travels through the Great Lakes because of all the industry along the shores. We could see smoke stacks in the towns as we passed by their shores. I had never thought about how much we depend on the river systems for transportation of goods.

Canada is on the starboard (right) side of the Saint Clair River; the United States is on the port (left) side. It's amazing to be able to see both countries from the boat while traveling the waterway.

We went up the Black River, pulled into the Port Huron city dock at 3:30 p.m., and checked in at the office. College kids were working here, and the young man helping us noticed we were "Hoosiers." He said "Hoosiers" were okay, but not Ohio. The "Buckeyes" are Michigan's rivals. So Captain P proceeded to tell him the joke about the buckeye—that it is just a worthless nut. The boy burst out laughing and said, "Man, I'm going to use that at our next game." Joe had a lot of fun talking with him about basketball.

It took 7 hours 45 minutes to get up the river to Port Huron because of the current we fought all day. The Captain says we have reached the halfway point of the journey of 2,531 miles.

We traveled 35.5 miles today.

Wednesday, July 23, 2003

Leaving our slip at the city dock at 7:00 a.m., we headed back to the Black River, which drains into the Saint Clair River. As we went upstream, the river narrowed, making the current very strong under the bridge. It looked like rapids at the bridge; Joe had to fight the wheel to keep us going in the right direction. The fellow at the SCYC marina had warned Joe about the strong current under the bridge. He advised Joe to stay on the Canadian side until we were through the bridge and then give the boat a little more horsepower. Joe followed the advice, and it worked just like the fellow said. This is where Lake Huron drains into St. Clair River, and the current is really swift.

We had a strong wind with four-foot seas, making it a rough ride—much like riding a bucking horse. You just hold on till you get through it. We went like this for five hours until we finally reached Port Sanilac at 12:30 p.m. We called it a day; we are getting too old for this rough stuff!

The wind had picked up and the sea was breaking over the top of the cabin. And I'm sitting in this boat! Of course, Joe was inside steering, but the waves were actually going over the pilothouse. Even Joe was glad to get into a safe harbor.

The little town of Sanilac was just up the hill from the marina. Only one restaurant and one hardware store were open. Joe wanted to buy a board to tie down the gas cans. They had moved around so much as we went through the rough water that we were afraid we might lose them overboard. We bought some pieces of cedar because that wouldn't rot in the sun and water.

After returning to the boat, I fixed dinner while Joe decided how to design the boards for the gas cans. We were trying to get in 63 miles today and get to Harbor Beach. Again, the weather did not cooperate.

A good thing about the east coast of Michigan is that a safe harbor can be found every 30 miles. The west coast is working to do the same. This is good news for all boaters.

The marinas in Michigan are all owned by the state and are priced very reasonably. Traveling by boat is very enjoyable through here.

We traveled 33.1 miles today.

Thursday, July 24, 2003

We left the dock at Port Sanilac and headed back into Lake Huron on our way to Harbor Beach. The day was beautiful and the water was good until 11:00. The wind started to pick up out of the northeast, making the water rough to navigate.

We pulled into Harbor Beach at 12:30 p.m. and tied behind the breakwater. An old abandoned lighthouse stood at the entrance to the harbor. It was calm here; I could relax and read. Joe finished cutting the boards to size and got the fuel cans secured. Now we won't have to worry about them jumping overboard.

After getting all that done, we went exploring. We climbed off the boat out on the breakwater and checked out the old lighthouse. As we looked out over the lake, we could see the water had calmed, but it was too late to go back out. So we stayed here and had a relaxing afternoon together. The sun was shining, a gentle breeze was blowing, and no one else was around. It was just the captain and I (let your imagination run wild)—now this is boating!

We traveled 29.9 miles today.

Friday, July 25, 2003

Up and out at 6:30 a.m., we saw a beautiful sunrise on the lake. Wind coming into the harbor all night made the boat rock and caused us not to get a very good night's sleep.

We headed for Harrisburg, Michigan, but first we had to cross Saginaw Bay, which is 26 miles across. The wind picked up, coming across our beam and causing choppy four-foot seas. Our boat was tossed around, making it an uncomfortable crossing. It was a nice sunny day, but just a little too windy.

Joe was getting tired, but we made it into the Harrisburg Marina harbor and anchored at 4:30 p.m. Ten hours on the water makes for a long day.

We are trying to get to Muskegon to meet some friends from our hometown in Indiana who will be there the first week of August. We don't know yet if we are going to make it, but Joe is trying really hard to make it for me.

We traveled 68.6 miles today.

Saturday, July 26, 2003

We stayed anchored at Harrisburg because of high winds and the possibility of a thunderstorm. Thank goodness, we have only had a lot of wind but no bad storms.

The Michigan coastline along here is mostly flat and covered with trees. We can see a few lake homes tucked back in the trees along the sandy coastline. This stretch of Michigan is not very populated.

Joe got some much needed rest and relaxation. The rain is pouring down, and we are glad to be in here and not out on the open water. It's as though Mother Nature doesn't want us to get to Muskegon while our friends are there. I think we will win unless something really nasty comes along on the waterway. Joe is determined to try to get us there on time.

Sunday, July 27, 2003

After getting a good rest yesterday, we were up and off this morning at 6:30 a.m. after enjoying another beautiful sunrise.

The water looked calm, so we headed for Presque Isle, a 65-mile run. At 8:30 the wind picked up, causing some good sized waves on the beam, making the boat list which means to tilt to one side. The waves came at a steady pace and made it difficult to keep on course. Joe had had enough, so we headed into the wind.

At 10:00 we turned into Thunder Bay, fighting the waves all the way in. Going ten miles out of our way to Alpena Marine Harbor, we arrived at 11:30. With the wind and waves, it took us a while to get back there.

After getting to the marina, we fueled up, pumped out the holding tank, docked the boat, and found out this was the last day for the Brown Trout Festival fishing tournament. The tournament was down to the finals. We went to check out the winning fish and to see what all the excitement was about.

They were catching Brown Trout and King Salmon; these fish are unbelievable. We stayed to watch them clean a few. The delicious looking fillet steaks made our mouths water!

The fish cleaning facility here is very nice, all stainless steel, and shiny as a new nickel.

Town is just up the hill, and after showering we walked there. We found a huge antique store and a restaurant, called J.J.'s, which had the best beer batter cod sandwiches ever. The sandwiches were so big that we took part of them with us to have for lunch tomorrow. I love leftovers!

The restaurant was decorated with stuffed wild animals, some in display cases and some on wall shelves. A full grown stuffed tiger was enclosed in glass—an awesome sight.

As we walked back through town to return to the boat, we found antique stores we will visit tomorrow.

While relaxing on the boat, we could hear a polka band playing under a tent in the parking lot. From the "hooting and hollering," it seemed they were having a great time. Polka music is happy music, and they were also playing some country and western. Polka country music—now that's different!

We traveled 33.2 miles today.

Monday, July 28, 2003

We got up this morning to strong north winds. There is a prediction of 5-10 mph west to southwest winds tomorrow. We will keep our fingers crossed for this much better forecast.

We walked nine blocks through town looking for a hardware store, but had no luck. We did, however, find a bookstore. Inside we met a well read gentleman, smoking a cigar, and looking for someone to sit a spell and chew the fat. Joe filled the bill while I browsed around.

I looked through the shelves of books that went from the floor to the ceiling while Joe talked the guy's ear off. They talked about boats and pipes. The store was so dark that I could hardly read the book titles. The owner wanted me to take more books than what I had selected. Since they were free, I wish I could have found more that interested me; but I thought I was going to go blind trying to read the titles as it was. He had just received more books from a local library and didn't have any place to put them. He showed us some painting he had done; he was a very talented man. We found him quite interesting. I know we were in the store an hour or so.

On the way back, we stopped at a dollar store before picking up some groceries. Getting back to the boat, we spent the evening relaxing.

This was a day of fun!

Tuesday, July 29, 2003

We left the dock this morning at 6:30; we had to retrace the ten miles we had come from the entrance to Thunder Bay. It was a beautiful day with very little wind. Heading north past Presque Isle to Rogers City, we saw some old abandoned lighthouses on the shore. I wish we had been close enough for me to take some pictures.

Prayers are answered; we finally have sunshine and calm water. This has been our first good day on Lake Huron. It was wonderful.

We pulled into Rogers City at 2:45 p.m. to a beautiful marina; it is clean and friendly. Would you believe that there is also a festival going on here? There are bands playing, rides, cotton candy, ice cream, and lots of people walking around. How lucky can we get?

The water along the coastline was full of fishermen. Every morning when we head out, the water is full of people fishing. It's that time of year for fun and fishing, and the tournaments are for serious money.

After we tied up to the dock, we went to town, walked around the fair and over to the IGA for supplies. We have a cold plate refrigeration on board, which usually works out rather well, but the ice lasts only about three days. By the time we need ice, we also need bread and milk, fruit and meat. The grocery store here is really boat friendly. We could take the grocery cart loaded with groceries back to the marina, and the next day someone from the grocery will pick it up. This was a welcomed convenience.

After putting away the supplies, we watched people walking around looking at the boats. All the marinas have people who seem to enjoy just observing the boats that are docked there. We can either draw our curtains, or we can smile and wave at them. Sometimes Joe goes out to talk with them. I am usually sitting at the table or fixing dinner.

Joe changed the oil at this stop.

We traveled 58 miles today.

Wednesday, July 30, 2003

There was a beautiful sunrise when we left the dock at Rogers City at 6:30 a.m. and headed back out to Lake Huron. The sky was full of dark clouds; but in the direction we were going, we saw a bright spot in the sky, a sign from above that someone is watching over us. At 8:30 we got a little rain with a light, variable wind and one-foot seas. We like these conditions; they are perfect for boating.

Grateful for the calm day, we passed Hammond Bay and decided to go on past Cheboygan, Michigan, since we were having such a great day.

Eight swans swam across the front of the boat in the South Channel between Cheboygan and Bois Blanc Island. They made such a graceful sight on the water.

Two big lake ships passed us, but we didn't get any wakes from them. We still get a funny feeling when we see those big ships.

At 11:45 we were headed for Mackinaw City, Michigan; we hoped to be there in two hours. We had a good day on Lake Huron, but we had to stop for a ferryboat crossing the Lake. It was interesting to watch how the cars were loaded on the ferry, which had room for only a few cars at a time. Imagine having to do this every morning to cross from the island to the mainland to go to work. I would guess that extra time would have to be allowed and lots of patience would be needed. The ferry is the only way to get across.

At noon, the sun had finally come out and we could see the Mackinac Bridge about 20 miles ahead. At 2:30 we pulled into the marina at Mackinaw City. The big shuttles that take people to the island are located here in this marina, so we don't have to walk far to get to them. From our boat we could see them and watch them turn within their own length. The captains turn them around to get ready to take the next group over to the island.

This is a tourist town, and there are many shops to explore. There is something here for every age. Everything is within walking distance of the marina. This is a great place to visit and a wonderful place for a family vacation. At this time of year many people are here; therefore, we will have to get going early in the morning to catch the shuttle. We want to be able to spend the whole day on the island.

We traveled 52.2 miles today.

Thursday, July 31, 2003

After breakfast we went over to the shuttle, which would take us to Mackinac Island. I was excited; we were going early and would spend the whole day. It would be so much fun.

It was a 16-minute ride to the island on the double-deck shuttle. Those sitting on the top deck received spray off the rooster tail, but they also had a fantastic view of the straits and the water. It went past the Round Island Lighthouse. I could get some good pictures from up there.

There are no motorized vehicles allowed on the island, according to the brochure. Everything is horse drawn; of course, Joe would spot the only tractor on the island. It was hauling gravel; maybe a tractor doesn't count because its help is needed.

Bicycles can be rented to help in getting around the island. Instead, we took the horse drawn carriage ride with a guide explaining all about the town's history. Stops are made that permit time to look around places such as the butterfly house, a blacksmith shop, Fort Mackinac, and the Governor's Mansion. We had time to walk, look around, and take pictures.

It is such an interesting place. With the yards full of beautiful flowers, stone animals hiding in flower beds, and homes with flower lined white picket fences, it is a photographer's dream.

The hotel on the main street has hanging baskets of greenery all across its balcony. Everything looked like a picture postcard.

After the carriage ride, we walked around town, went through more shops, had lunch, and took lots of pictures. There is a fudge shop on every corner; in fact, we were told that tourists are called "fudgies." I was proud of myself; I didn't buy any fudge, but the aroma didn't make it easy. Fans blew that wonderful fudge aroma out on the sidewalk to tempt weak souls.

At 7:30 we were back on the shuttle going back to the main island. We walked back to our boat after spending a wonderful day together while learning the history of the island. I'm really glad we were able to stop here. It has been a great day.

We heard thunder off in the distance, and it looks like a storm is moving in. The wind is picking up. I'm glad it waited so we could enjoy the day and get back to the boat.

We both enjoyed today; I recommend a visit to Mackinac Island.

Friday, August 1, 2003

We awoke to a rainy morning. According to the weather station, storms could be expected throughout the day. We decided we would stay here at the Mackinaw marina for at least one more day. The marina is very clean and has nice facilities. The dock master is very knowledgeable, and college kids are working in the office.

Staying here another day has given us time to talk with some of the other boaters. As we roamed around the docks, some asked about the Florida registration on the side of "Whoosher." Others wanted to know what kind of boat she is. Most can't believe we came all the way from Florida by boat. When they find out we are doing the loop, they are full of more questions. Maybe we will get someone else enthused about doing the loop also.

It's always interesting to talk with other boaters to find out where they are headed. I like to get ideas on cooking meals on board.

Up and down the dock we see families pushing strollers, people walking their dogs, and couples walking hand in hand. Some stopped to look at our little boat.

Having done the laundry, we walked to town for dinner at The Family Restaurant, where we had Alaskan Pollack with mashed potatoes and gravy, slaw, and rolls. Good!

After dinner we walked a few blocks to the IGA to buy supplies. This little grocery was the only one around and their prices were a little high. We bought only the necessities.

Joe made coffee for morning after we got back to the boat. We decided that because the evening was so nice we would walk back to town, so off we went, hand in hand. We treated ourselves to raspberry truffle and vanilla ice cream in waffle cones. You know who got the raspberry! Oh my gosh, I wish you could have had a taste of this. It was Sooo Goood!!

We turned in early after getting back to the boat. We hope to get an early start as we continue The Loop. We will finally be going south, toward our destination of Florida!

Saturday, August 2, 2003

We left at 6:30 a.m. with fog and a half-mile visibility. Joe said we were going anyway. Getting out into the harbor and under the Mackinac Bridge was a little scary. It was so foggy that we couldn't see; thank God for the GPS.

Lake Michigan glimmered like glass; it was calm and smooth. It stayed like this all day with only a ripple from sport fishermen going past. It was mostly hazy all day; however, a little sunshine peeked through once in a while. Over all, it was not a bad day.

At 3:10 we pulled into Charlevoix, Michigan. Charlevoix is reached by going back on the Pine River, under a bascule bridge, and into Round Lake, which will take you back into Lake Charlevoix. We anchored for the night in Round Lake after having a good day on the water.

We had dinner on board and relaxed out in the cockpit; more curious boaters were out looking at the boat. This is a really nice, safe anchorage that is surrounded by trees. There is some boat traffic going back and forth to Lake Charlevoix. It's fun to watch them as they look us over.

We traveled 58.2 miles today.

Sunday, August 3, 2003

Several fishermen were already out when we left Charlevoix at 6:30 a.m. The morning was cloudy, but the water was calm. The sky looked a bit stormy; but by the time we got to Leland, Michigan, around noon, it was blue skies and bright sunshine. The decision was made to go ahead to Frankfort, Michigan, forty miles away. It's that window of opportunity again.

The west coast of Michigan is like one big sand dune created by Mother Nature. The largest of all the dunes, called The Sleeping Bear, is 400 feet high. This is a huge pile of sand!

The storm clouds went around us, and we got to Frankfort at 5:30. After Joe caught his breath, we walked to town and found a restaurant called Dinghy's. This was evidently the place to be for everyone in town; it was crowded and every seat was taken. Finally, we were able to get a booth and sit down. It was obvious we were in a boating town on the water because of the clever decorations. Several old wood plaques on the wall had sayings like "Sailors don't die, they just get a little dinghy" and "Old sailors never die; they just smell that way." I would bet this place is crazy after the dinner hour.

We ordered a blooming onion for an appetizer and hamburgers and French fries for dinner. Again, we ate too much, but we were having a good time and the food was good.

Since leaving Detroit about two weeks ago, we have not been able to use our cell phone. We miss talking to everyone. Our granddaughter Jada left a voice mail, and it did my ole' heart good just to hear her voice.

This has been a delightful day with calm winds and seas.

We traveled 74.1 miles today.

Monday, August 4, 2003

As we left the Frankfort dock at 7:00 a.m., we already had one-foot seas. There were more sand dunes along the shores of Michigan, but we could not see any towns—just sand as far as we could see.

The sea was getting rougher the closer we got to Manistee, Michigan, with the wind coming from the northwest. We were glad to get into port.

We arrived in Manistee at 11:00, but we had to get fuel before getting into our slip. We needed to relax a while after fighting the waves. We checked in at the office and then walked to town, which was just up the hill to the left. After walking all the way through town, we finally found a store where we could get film developed. I had seven rolls to develop; I can't wait to see the pictures.

By getting to the marina early, we had plenty of time to walk around town. In an antique store I found a heart-shaped pendant to wear on a gold chain. This is another souvenir I will take home as a reminder of our trip.

By the time we picked up the pictures and got back to the boat, Joe was exhausted. By the time I fixed dinner and we relaxed a bit, he had gotten his second wind and we took a walk.

We walked back to town and picked up some supplies at the local grocery. Doesn't it seem like we are always getting groceries and supplies? We just happened to walk past an ice cream shop—one of Joe's weaknesses. We treated ourselves to Mackinac Island fudge and vanilla in waffle cones. This was good stuff!

We took the canal river walk back to the boat. The sidewalk along the canal took us back to the marina; benches invited us to stop to enjoy the water and the flowers that were blooming. The town is boat friendly and very pretty.

The wind is not cooperating with us; it is blowing from the wrong direction and it looks like we may be here for a while. Lake Michigan can be rough when the wind comes from the northwest. We hope it changes and calms down so we can move on.

We traveled 28.8 miles today.

Tuesday, August 5, 2003

There was a 5-10 mph northwest wind when we left at 7:00 a.m. It was calm, but a little cloudy.

A tall ship passed by us; this is quite a sight out on the open water. There was not much to see while going down this coast—just sand dunes and water. It was really peaceful out there; the water calmly pushes you along ever so gently, up and down with each wave. There weren't even any sport fishermen going around us churning up the water today. I sat out in the cockpit and enjoyed the ride. Joe let Popeye do the steering for a while to give him a much-needed rest. It's about time Popeye paid his way. This is what he is supposed to do, and this calm water was perfect for the autopilot. I'm glad Joe figured it out in time.

We anchored at Pentwater Lake at noon after a good day on the water. I fixed a spaghetti dinner. Getting to the anchorage early gave Joe time to work on the stove and cockpit seats.

There is always something to do on the boat, just like at home. You fix one thing and two more break. There was not much I could do while he had the floor open to the bilge. I couldn't tidy up until he was done working. This was my time to read or listen to CD's and just chill out. This works out, and everyone stays happy.

We traveled 38 miles today.

Wednesday, August 6, 2003

We awoke to dense fog and had to wait for Mr. Sunshine to rise and burn off some of it before we could continue our journey south. We finally pulled anchor at 7:15 a.m. The fog tried to hang on, but the sun won out and the rest of the day was beautiful and sunny.

Getting into the harbor at Muskegon, Michigan, we docked at Hartshorne Municipal Marina at 2:00 p.m. When we checked in at the office, we asked the office manager if there was a good place to eat nearby. He told us the best pizza place in town just happened to be right across from the marina parking lot in an old warehouse that had been refurbished.

After showering, we went to Fricano's Pizza Parlor to celebrate 3,000 miles on the water and the fact that we were still married and talking to each other. This is a miracle in itself after living in a 31 by 11 foot room. Sometimes, it's like we are connected at the hip; at other times, things get a little testy. He says he has a big responsibility because the grandkids' Nannie is on board.

Taking the long way back to the boat to exercise and work off the pizza, we found out that 11 tall ships are coming to a festival this weekend. This will be at the park located next to the marina.

The tall ships are sailing here from all around the world, and to be able to see them up close will be awesome. Tickets to board the ships can be purchased. The captains and crews will be available to answer questions. This should be an interesting experience.

We have arrived here in time to meet up with our good friends from Shoals, Indiana. We are going to call them this evening to let them know we made it. When we were home over the Fourth of July, they told us they were going to be here the first week of August. We told them we would try to get here at the same time.

When we talked to Michael, he insisted on coming over to the marina to take us to their rental vacation house to visit for a while this evening. It was nice to see all their friendly faces. Mike and Kathy had their whole crew with them: their daughter Amy, her husband Brent, and their children, Katelynn, Summer Rose, and David; and their son Jonathan and his girlfriend. Their other daughter Jenny had already left to go back home. They have been here for a few days already having a good time. Joe had some ice cream on one of Kathy's freshly baked brownies. This was a real treat for Joe because Kathy makes good brownies, and we know about him and his ice cream!

We enjoyed the evening visiting with everyone. Mike took us back to the boat, and we made plans to get together the next day to do something. They offered to take us to the store or wherever else we needed to go. They are the best!

We traveled 47.6 miles today.

Thursday, August 7, 2003

fter a wonderful evening with Mike, Kathy, and their gang, we were up having coffee and breakfast. They said they would be over this morning to take us to a local Meijer's store so we could pick up supplies. It was nice of them to offer to do this because it is much easier than trying to catch a bus to go buy supplies. I made my list of the things we needed.

It has been a wonderful day here; there has been a refreshing breeze blowing. I watched a small turtle feeding in the water beside the boat. For some reason, I haven't seen very many turtles on our trip.

Mike and Kathy arrived with the whole clan. They wanted a tour of the boat both inside and out. We had to keep everybody moving; there's not enough room for nine people on the boat at one time.

I think they were surprised at the boat's compactness and its constant movement, which takes some getting used to. Kathy got a little seasick, so they didn't stay on the boat very long.

We piled into their two vans and took off shopping. It's nice to get off the boat and walk, but it was fun being together with their family. They have a nice group of kids.

While on the waterway before getting to Muskegon, we had a sport fisherman go around us making a big wake. It knocked our little AC/DC TV off the shelf and broke it. We tried to find another one, but didn't have any luck finding a 13-inch replacement. Thinking we probably wouldn't get any reception while going down the river system, we decided not to get one right now.

Michael took all of us to dinner at Ruby Tuesday's—his treat. (We owe them a dinner.) We had a wonderful dinner and a great time with everyone. It was wonderful of them to include us in their family vacation for a couple of days. We really enjoyed being with them. We miss our family and kids back home. Thank you, Mike and Kathy.

Friday, August 8, 2003

The forecast this morning was for 2-4 foot seas; it would be too windy for us to be out on Lake Michigan. Joe worked on the boat this morning cleaning the cockpit and checking the engine.

Mike and Kathy came by on their way over to the tall ships. We started getting ready to go, but a little shower popped up. We went over after the rain stopped, but we missed seeing Mike and Kathy.

We lucked out by being in Muskegon at the same time the tall ships were there. Getting to see them come into the harbor earlier with their sails up was a sight that few people get to see. Seeing them up close was a real treat. These boats remind you of the time of pirates; they are different from the ships we saw in Sandusky, Ohio.

After looking at all the ships, we walked over to the great pizza parlor again. Actually, it was the only place to eat within walking distance unless we caught a bus—and it was good pizza. We haven't had pizza since New York. They had only one size of pizza available, but you could order it any way you wanted it and all at one price. Needless to say, they were busy.

As we walked a few blocks to work off some of our dinner, we passed some big old homes that could be toured. I would have liked touring them, but we will be leaving tomorrow.

We returned to the marina to find Mike and Kathy pulling out of the parking lot. We told them we are leaving tomorrow, weather permitting, and they are going to leave Saturday as well. This has worked out great—we had some time off and got to visit with friends at the same time.

Now, back to completing the task we started on April 19, The Great Circle.

Saturday, August 9, 2003

After breakfast we took our showers. The office was late in opening and we had to wait to turn in the security key, but we are finally headed south again.

We crossed our fingers wishing for a good day on the water. A little wind can cause this lake to turn on you in a heartbeat, and you don't want to get caught miles offshore with no safe anchorages on the west coast of Michigan. Supposedly, the anchorage problem is being worked on; it will be nice for boaters when this is done.

The day went well until later in the afternoon. We started getting 2-3 foot seas, which was not too bad with the wind on the stern (back), but it was hard for Joe to stay on course.

In addition to the wind, we had to dodge fish traps and fishing boats. We went through a sailboat racecourse which had been set up out in the lake. It was tricky going through that and not getting in their way.

We saw a few sailboats going our way, as well as some big lake ships off in the distance headed for Canada across the Great Lakes.

At 5:45 p.m. we arrived in South Haven after putting in more than eight hours on the water. We were tired, but it was a good tired. We docked at the South Haven Marina and checked in at the office. We were here ten years ago to take a navigational course on sailing. It would help me learn how to handle a sailboat and determine if I would get seasick doing so. I passed both categories with flying colors.

We wanted to find the same fish and chips place where we ate back then, but everything had changed. We think we found the location, but it wasn't the same name. We had a fish and chips dinner at Captain Lou's and then walked around town.

This is the blueberry capital of the world, and blueberries are shipped all over the world from here. A blueberry festival was going on, and everything that can be made from the fruit was available. The delicious smells were so tempting! I understand that blueberries make you happy—it worked for me!

We stopped at a shop to get blueberry muffins for breakfast only to find out they were all sold out. Instead, Joe had vanilla ice cream in a big waffle cone and ate it as we walked back to the boat.

As we went back on board "Whoosher," our neighbors in the slip next to ours were sitting out in their cockpit. They wanted to know about the boat and asked about coming up the east coast from Florida. Joe told them what we are doing, and they thought it was fantastic. They had questions about the Loop; they hope to do it someday and were interested in knowing about it.

In talking to them, we discovered they were fellow Hoosiers from Nappanee, Indiana. We had an enjoyable evening talking to them till 10:30. We could have talked longer, but it was getting late and we were tired.

We traveled 64.2 miles today.

Sunday, August 10, 2003

We left the dock at 7:00 a.m. with sunshine burning off the fog early this morning. The forecast was 1-2 foot seas with wind out of the northwest. This was not good, but we went anyway.

After getting out in the lake, we found the biggest two-foot seas we've seen. It was hard to hold the boat on course. Keeping a firm grip on the wheel for hours makes for a tired captain. When the water is rough, the autopilot doesn't help much because the boat is tossed around so much by the waves that it can't hold the course.

After seeing nothing but water for miles, we finally pulled into Michigan City, Indiana, at 3:30 p.m., getting us closer to home. We fueled up and tied up in a slip. This is the marina we left from when we took the navigation course ten years ago. It didn't look a thing like it did then, but then neither do I look like I did ten years ago.

We knew town was within walking distance, so we took off across the park and across the bridge to town. We had a hamburger, fries, onion rings, and iced tea at Swingbelly's, a restaurant renovated from an old railroad station. Some of the old walls and railroad lights had been used as decorations.

This marina has very nice facilities with a laundry, sandwich shop, and security fence for the boats. I did laundry when we got back, showered, and relaxed the rest of the evening.

After living on a boat like this, you realize how little you need to survive and be happy. What really matters is being thankful for each day you are given.

We called Rodger and Dee and Mark and Trish. We could finally use our cell phone again (yeah!). Rodger is keeping track of us with maps of The Loop. They are always interested in knowing how far we have gotten and how we are doing. It seems that we are living the dream of several people in the adventure of The Great Circle!

We traveled 58.2 miles today.

Monday, August 11, 2003

This was another cloudy day with 35-knot winds out of the northeast; 5-8 foot seas were predicted. These are not good conditions for trying to cross Lake Michigan to Chicago on a 31-foot sailboat. We will stay here in Michigan City until the weather changes.

After we get across the lake to Chicago, we will start in the river systems. Not having all the charts we need, I called the Army Corps of Engineers to order what we need. They will be sent here "next day air" so we can look them over and be ready to leave as soon as the weather cooperates.

We walked to the big outlet mall located a few blocks from here. I hoped to pick up some Christmas gifts because I will be getting a late start this year with my shopping.

There was a Big Dog Shop, and I was able to mark a few kids off my list there. I found some really cute things that I couldn't resist. Joe tried to find some shoes, but there was nothing in his size.

When the wind became a little nippy, we headed back to the marina, first stopping at the Galveston Steak Restaurant for dinner. I ordered a steak and Joe had chicken; both were very good. Joe made coffee when we were back on the boat, and that warmed up the boat a bit. It's chilly tonight.

It's sad to see downtown Michigan City looking like a ghost town with so many of its buildings deserted. Everything has moved out to the big highway.

When we walked to the mall, we saw a beautiful old church. This is another historic town with interesting homes. We love walking through the towns, plus it gives us needed exercise.

The wind is supposed to go to the southeast Wednesday or Thursday. Maybe we will be able to continue south by then. It is nice to get a rest, but we are ready to get going. I hope the charts come in tomorrow because we will need them to navigate down the rivers.

Tuesday, August 12, 2003

It was really windy today. After breakfast we walked out to the entrance of the marina to watch the waves coming over the breakwater at the marina's entrance. Seeing the waves crashing against the big boulders and coming over the cement wall was quite a sight. Waves rolled in on the beach as well, and we had to be careful not to get wet. The spray from the wind was enough to dampen our clothes. We saw several boats try to go out, but they came right back. The waves just about swallowed them when they got out from behind the breakwater. That was scary to watch.

We returned to the boat to find that the maps we had ordered had arrived. We looked through them; they were not exactly what Joe wanted, but they will work. They will get us down the river system and show us water depths and anchorages. This is all we need to know; all we have to do is stay between the banks for the most part.

Joe changed the oil, filter, and the fuel filters. He's still killing spiders; I'm not sure we will ever get rid of all of them. We are anxious to get going as soon as the weather cooperates.

We asked the dock master about the nearest grocery store and directions to get to it. We would have to take a bus to the other side of town in order to do any shopping. Now I know where all the stores went! When we went to the outlet mall the other day, we walked past the bus stop up by the library about two blocks away. Taking the bus wasn't easy, but without transportation we had no other choice. According to the maps, once we start down the river system there is no place to stop for supplies. Also, there are not many anchorages for quite a distance.

This was not a good day for walking anywhere. It was windy and cool, but it is August and fall is already in the air up here. We had to get supplies in before leaving here, or we would be going hungry.

So often on this trip we have known that a higher power is looking over us. Once again, we were rescued. Ron, the gas dock master came by the boat to tell us he was headed home. If we wanted, he would drop us off at Meijer's and then bring us back to the marina. We couldn't believe our ears; we grabbed our coats and headed out with Ron.

He stopped at a CVS pharmacy so I could get our medicine refilled, and then he took us to Meijer's. He gave us his phone number, told us to take our time, and then call him when we were ready to go back. He pointed out some restaurants where we could get dinner.

We couldn't believe our luck! We finished shopping for supplies and had a hamburger and fries at the restaurant in the grocery store. We sat there just counting our blessings. We called Ron, who met us out front and took us back to the marina. He refused to take anything for being so nice. He told us to pass it on and help someone else along our way. God is looking out for us!

Wednesday, August 13, 2003

Today has been nice with sunshine; it was a little breezy, but conditions have improved.

We walked over to the original Michigan City Lighthouse that once stood at the entrance to the harbor for over 100 years. It has been restored and turned into a museum for tourists to enjoy. Sand dunes were leveled to provide a site for the park and marina. The guide taking us through the museum obviously loved his work and had many interesting stories to share. Models of old ships, including the first submarine, were on display. An old prism light from the first lighthouse was cut in half to show how the formation of the glass makes a small bulb give a bigger and brighter light. This prism light is called a Fresnell lens, named after the man who invented it. Pictures of the river and of the town when it was first built also contributed to an interesting and educational tour appropriate for all ages. We were fascinated by all of the history found in the museum.

We walked to the post office to mail some postcards and then went back to the outlet mall, which is the only place within walking distance for shopping. While I went into a bookstore to look around, Joe sat on a park bench smoking his pipe. I overheard some ladies in the bookstore talking about the man sitting on the bench smoking his pipe. I think they were admiring my husband.

We ate at the Pullman Café where we enjoyed a very good whitefish, mashed potatoes, and corn dinner with iced tea.

Trains were very important here at one time, a fact that may have inspired the decorating theme in this section of the shopping center. A piece of the old train tracks and wheels from a train could be examined here.

After getting back to the boat, Joe made coffee, and we got everything ready so we can leave in the morning. The winds are to be out of the east going southeast with no more than 2-foot seas. It looks good for boating. We have been here five days, and we are ready to get moving.

CHAPTER 4

RIVER SYSTEM
CHICAGO, ILL. - - - MOBILE, ALABA

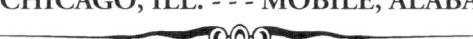

Thursday, August 14, 2003

At 7:00 a.m. we left the marina at Michigan City, Indiana, going from the lower end of Lake Michigan and heading to Chicago, Illinois. We wanted to anchor along Lakeshore Drive, which runs along the skyline of the Chicago waterfront. (We anchored there ten years ago on our sailboat navigation course. It was an awesome sight at night seeing the buildings lit up.) We had a little fog and one-foot seas; the wind started southeast and went north, nothing like what was predicted. We rolled a little, but not too badly. According to the radio, the weather was changing from west to northwest. Once out in the water, you have to handle the seas or turn around and go back.

Heading into the Chicago harbor, we were met by the coast guard telling us the harbor was closed. We were not sure why it was closed, but you don't argue with the coast guard. We really had set our hearts on anchoring there so we could get pictures of the harbor lit up at night. When we were here before, we didn't get to do so. The reflections the lighted buildings made in the water were something we wanted to experience again. But since we couldn't anchor there, we went to plan B.

On shore along the harbor seawall, there was a fair with rides going on. The tall ships, Windy I and Windy II, were tied up at the docks taking people for rides out in the harbor.

Not knowing where else to go to anchor for the night, we went on through the Chicago Harbor Lock and on down the Illinois River, a 327-mile system that ends where it joins the Mississippi River at Grafton, Illinois. This makes up the Chicago Sanitary Canal, the largest canal built in the 19th century. It is 12 feet deep and runs from Chicago to Lockport.

Anyone entering the Chicago locks must be wearing a life jacket. We had not had to wear them to go through any of the locks up until now, but we were told right away to get them on before going through.

The Chicago Sanitary Canal goes through the middle of downtown Chicago. We could see people looking out their office windows. Some were walking across the bridge or just standing on it looking at boat traffic passing under; perhaps they were taking a break from the office. Some of the office buildings had balconies with large pots of flowers and hanging baskets with vines trailing from them. We passed other tall buildings, including the Sun-Times and Sears Tower. It was a treat to see them from the boat.

After getting through the downtown area and starting down the river, we began seeing petroleum tanks and industrial areas. Barges, some of them waiting to be loaded, were being pushed to their destinations by towboats. Towboats on the Illinois River must have retractable pilothouses in order to pass under bridges on the upper portion of the river, beginning with the swing bridge at Romeoville. The pilothouses were raised and lowered by hydraulic rams. We just got over, stayed out of their way, and let them go around us.

We had to wait to get through the locks at Lockport, Illinois, because the barges have the right of way. At 8:00 p.m. we stopped for the night at Joliet. We had been going for 13 hours and were really tired and ready to stop for the night. We tied up to a wall that was right in town.

We couldn't escape the turbulence from the towboats that passed by all night and rocked us around. Getting farther down the river would have been better, and getting out of the channel would have been better still.

We did get to see a towboat lower its pilothouse to get under the bridge in Joliet. It reminded me of E.T. (extra-terrestrial).

I made a quick chicken salad, which we ate out in the cockpit listening to music from speakers located in the park next to us. The music came from live entertainment at Harrah's Casino across the river from us. We just relaxed and enjoyed the music.

Joe had to adjust the idle, which was too slow. This is a no-wake zone, which means boats must go slowly so they do not make waves. However, two boats went past and rocked us so badly that we had to grab our plates to keep them from being thrown to the floor. Some boaters have no respect for other boaters.

We made up some of the time we lost from staying in Michigan City because of the weather, but it certainly made a long day.

We traveled 83.5 miles today.

Friday, August 15, 2003

We headed out at 9:00 a.m. after spending a rocky night because of the waves made by all the towboats as they passed by. We headed toward Brandon Road Lock two miles down the canal, the second lock in the Chicago water system (have your life jackets on).

This is a busy canal with lots of barge traffic. The locks here are 600 by 110 feet, big enough for tows with wide loads to go through. It took a while to get locked through because of the time needed to fill the lock. It was 10:00 a.m. before we got through the locks.

We arrived at the Dresden Island Locks at noon. We had to get out of the way of another tow that was three barges wide. The prop wash from these big boats pushed us around and out of the channel making it necessary to watch the depth gauge and keep a good grip on the wheel.

The Marseilles Locks were at miles 244. We looked for a place to stop at Ottawa; but finding nothing; we continued on and anchored behind Mayo Island at 5:45 p.m. We anchored behind a barge tied to the bank. Because there were several boats out playing around and creating waves, the barge protected us from the rocking they would have caused. This was a good spot.

Today we were in the Des Plaines River, the Kankakee River, and the Illinois River. We saw a deer in the water feeding on leaves from a limb over her head.

There are also seagulls and herons through here. It has been a good day.

We traveled 51 miles today.

Saturday, August 16, 2003

After a quiet peaceful night we took off at 7:00 a.m. after having coffee and blueberry muffins. With sunshine overhead, we continued south once again.

It was five miles to Starved Rock Lock. When we arrived there, we found one tow waiting to come up and two waiting to go down. The first tow didn't have a load, so he called the lockmaster to allow us to lock through with him. Tow captains have to OK a pleasure craft's going through the locks with them; we felt privileged to have this opportunity. It could have been a long day waiting for the barges to go through. It can take up to an hour for barges to lock through.

We called to thank the tow captain and discovered that he was going to Baton Rouge, Louisiana. He wished us a safe trip, and we did the same. Not all tow captains are so friendly.

Pleasure boaters were out today, passing us on the beam, waving and smiling. We had to tack back and forth to avoid being rocked badly. But that's the way it goes on nice days when you have to share the water with other boaters.

We passed the cliff named Starved Rock. It is a huge, almost barren island cliff surrounded by other cliffs covered with trees. Its barrenness makes it stand out from the others.

There are no anchorages with any depth along here, and the city docks get bad wakes from all the traffic. We got in behind a sunken barge just out of the channel; there was just enough water for us to get behind it. We did not get any wake from other boaters, making this a good anchorage.

This was the hottest day on the water that we have had so far; the temperature reached 90 degrees.

We stopped at 4:00 p.m. after traveling 58 miles today.

Sunday, August 17, 2003

The sun was burning off the fog this morning as we prepared to leave our anchorage after having a nice quiet night. At 8:30 we attempted to get out from behind the barge, and guess what? We are stuck. Joe climbed up on the old barge to push off just enough for us to get loose. He jumped back on while I kept us headed in the right direction. What a team we make!

We headed for Peoria Lock and Dam, but there was no place to tie up. So, we moved on and stopped at the Pekin Boat Club at 12:45 p.m. We had called ahead to see if the water depth was sufficient for us to get into their docks. They said the water was deep enough, but when we arrived we had to take the first spot at the dock where the depth was barely enough for us to get up to the dock. We are sure we are sitting on bottom. I hope the water doesn't go down any further.

It has been another really hot, humid day. After two 90-degree days we are ready for a shower and a good meal. We checked in at the Pekin Boat Club and Bar, reached by walking along the dock that had a 15-foot high bank, with a campground on top.

At the office we asked about the water level and were told that just last week the campground was flooded. We are glad we were not traveling through here at that time.

After showering, a big cool drink was in order. We went to the club for a Walleye dinner with shrimp and clams; it was yummy.

A local boater noticed that the registration on the side of our boat was from Florida. He asked if we had brought the boat all the way by water. When we told him we had, he announced it to the whole club and we became the center of attention. Asking us about the boat and the trip, they made us feel like celebrities. They wanted to know how, when, and where. Everyone gathered around to listen and ask more questions. They thought it was great that someone making The Loop had stopped in Pekin, Illinois.

One woman, who had her 90-year-old father with her, looked just like Olive Oyl, Popeye's girlfriend. She was infatuated with Joe, telling him she was waiting for a sailor to come along and take her away. I wasn't too worried; she wasn't Joe's type. She sure was giving him a sad tale. I hope she finds a Popeye of her own soon.

Then a young redheaded woman came over to our table, sat down, and talked our heads off. She told us to be sure to stop at the Alton Marina and that it was a five-star marina and would be the highlight of our trip. Five-star sounded expensive, but we told her we would check it out. She said to tell them she had sent us and to tell the staff hello for her. The name of her boat was "Fireball." If you could see her, you would know why.

We went only 25.6 miles today.

Monday, August 18, 2003

With a beautiful morning, we started down the Illinois River at 7:00 a.m. Going through some peaceful wilderness with a nice breeze blowing, we had easy cruising. There was no one else, just lots of birds, including two adult eagles perched in the top of a big old tree. It is wonderful seeing them out in the wild.

Stopping at Beardstown, we tied up our boat to the Welcome Barge and found we were within walking distance of town. A platform has been built here, providing a place to sit and enjoy the river on a nice evening. We had to check it out.

We ate at the Riverfront Restaurant. Built over a bowling alley right on the river, it was conveniently located by our boat. We enjoyed our dinner of Walleye fish, baked potato, salad bar, and iced tea.

After dinner we walked around town, stopping at a drug store for finger polish remover. Returning to the boat, we found a young man fishing off the barge and catching garfish. He told Joe they were not good to eat, and he kept throwing them back or stepping on them. (I'm not sure that's the way to kill a fish.)

We were already in bed when some teenagers climbed on top of the barge and dared each other to dive off. One by one, they jumped, laughing and having a good time as only teens can. I'm not sure they knew there was anyone on board the boat, or even if they cared. After they all took turns jumping, they left. This was a good stop.

We traveled 65 miles today.

Tuesday, August 19, 2003

Up early, we untied from the barge at 6:15 a.m. A tow with a load of barges was coming, and we wanted to get out in front so we could get through the locks ahead of it.

Heading for the LaGrange Locks, we called ahead; they were open and waiting for us. We sailed right through; and as soon as we got through, they closed them down for repair. Whew! That was luck.

We had the river all to ourselves again today; and when we got to the bridge at Hardin, Illinois, we found out why. The bridge was being worked on, and the barges couldn't get through. They were lined up along the bank for miles waiting for the okay to go through. I'm glad we didn't have to wait.

We saw a full-grown bald eagle again today. It was beautiful. So many kinds of wildlife enjoy the river; we always keep our eyes open so we don't miss any of it. We had just passed the sign to Michael, Illinois, when we saw the eagle.

Our plan was to stop in Hardin, Illinois, but Joe didn't like the wall we would have to tie up to. Instead, we continued to 12 Mile Island between Hardin and Grafton, and at 4:30 p.m. we anchored behind it. This is a nice anchorage back off the main water. Vacation cottages are built on one side, but it doesn't appear that anyone is living in them right now. Tired and hot, we ate out in the cockpit and relaxed after a sunny day on the water.

While we sat out in the cockpit, a humming bird came up behind me. It must have been attracted by the bright colors I was wearing. This has been another good day!

We traveled 76 miles today.

Wednesday, August 20, 2003

After coffee and hard-boiled eggs for breakfast, we were out of the anchorage at 8:00 a.m. We started off with sunshine and a warm breeze; birds sang all around us. That is always a good sign.

We began seeing small cottages along the banks. They were built high off the ground on stilts because there is always a good chance of flooding along the waterway.

At 9:45 a.m. we entered the Mississippi River with a southeast wind and one-foot caps. It is much wider than the Illinois River. Miles of granite bluffs appear on the Illinois side. We passed the Mark Twain National Wildlife Refuge. Everywhere there is a landscape of trees and flowers.

At 3:45 p.m. we pulled into the Alton Marina in Alton, Illinois. We stopped at the fuel dock first to get our slip number and noticed right away that all the slips here are under a roof. This is a great idea to get you out of the hot sunshine. We were feeling the effects of today's 97-degree temperature, and it was wonderful to be under the roof and out of the sun. Getting hooked up to the A/C, along with being under the roof, helped to cool the boat quickly.

Checking in at the office, we found the marina has a swimming pool, hot tub, and the most gorgeous showers we have seen at a marina. The shower rooms had rich mahogany walls, stacks of terry bath mats, a hair dryer, and containers of soap, shampoo, and conditioner in each shower. This is definitely a five-star marina. I know two ladies who vote that this is a definite stop.

Town is just up the hill and within walking distance. We had seen a casino from the river on our way to the marina. We were told at the office that the casino would send a car to pick us up and then return us to the marina. Just let the office know and they will call for the casino car.

Joe washed off the boat, and we both showered. I was starving, and I went to the office to have them call for the casino car, which delivered us to the casino. We walked two blocks up the hill to the Casa Margarita, a Mexican restaurant, which had very good food and authentically dressed waiters.

While enjoying our dinner, a waiter came out of the kitchen carrying five platters on his arm and lost his balance. The platters crashed to the floor, making a big mess. He turned right around, went back to the kitchen, came out with five more platters, and delivered them to the table, never missing a beat. The mess was all cleaned up in a few minutes. I was impressed.

As we walked through town, we noticed marks painted on the sides of buildings indicating the depth of floodwaters. It's unbelievable how high they were.

Since it was such a nice evening, we decided to walk back to the boat. The casino was all lit up, and the lights along the river were a pretty sight. The exercise also felt good. The boat was comfortably cool when we returned to it. It was still 83 degrees at 8:30 p.m.

Joe was tired, so he turned in while I did the laundry up behind the office. I love this place. I'm glad that lady back in Pekin told us about it. We have had another good day and evening together.

We traveled 27 miles today.

Thursday, August 21, 2003

We woke up to a cool boat (being under a roof helped), but it was already hot and humid outside. There was fog on the water, and we had to wait for it to clear before we could leave.

The Mel Price Lock #26 is two miles down from the Alton Marina. We could see the locks from our slip. There was one tow after another going through. We didn't want to get out to the lock and have to wait, so we called the lockmaster to ask him about locking through. He told us he would call us as soon as it was clear. This was so nice of him, especially when he was so busy.

We got ready so we could make the 15-20 minute trip to the lock quickly when he called back. At 10:00 he called to say we could lock

140

through, and at 10:45 we were through the Mel Price Lock and Dam and were on our way down the Mississippi River. There was a little turbulence at the Missouri River going into the Chain of Rocks Canal. We caught up with the tow and followed it until it stopped. We found out that the large locks were down for repair; however, we could lock through the small locks (thank goodness), but had to wait an hour. When we came back into the river, we picked up some current. It is hard to keep track of where we are because of the lack of names on river terminals.

We had the current with us today, so we made good time. It was hot, but we had a breeze, thank goodness. The temperature reached 102 degrees, and I spent a lot of the day lying down in the front cabin trying to stay cool. Wearing just my gauze cover-up, I poured water on my head to cool off. I should have been pouring water over Joe because he became dehydrated and started getting dizzy.

We stopped at a place called Hoppie's Marina outside Kimmswick, Missouri. There are not a lot of choices along here, and this was the only place to stop along this stretch of the Mississippi River. Fortunately, we were close to it because Joe needed to stop and rest quickly. Hoppie's is just a couple of barges tied together with a makeshift shelter that has a couch and chairs for protection from the sun. It is a little rough, but better than nothing. They did have electric hookup (sort of), but no showers or water. Thank God for the electricity.

After Joe was re-hydrated and the boat had cooled down, we walked up the hill to the little town of Kimmswick. It's mostly a tourist town with cute little cottages, small souvenir and craft shops, and eateries. At 3:00 everything was closed. Walking on through town, we came upon a beautiful old log house at the edge of town. It had become a restaurant, and it was still open. Real Indian teepees were set up in the front yard, but there were no Indians.

We went inside, asked the hostess if we could look around, and went upstairs to find more authentic Indian artifacts displayed on the walls—baby to full Indian feather headdresses, tools, weapons, furs, and handmade furniture.

Downstairs, the hostess seated us at a table with a blue/brown plaid tablecloth with matching napkins. She brought us water and handed us menus that looked like old parchment paper rolled up like a scroll and tied with twine. They were ingenious.

After looking over the menu, we ordered chicken breast smothered with broccoli and wine sauce, baked potato, green beans, and sweet tea. Included with dinner was homemade cornbread and butter.

We learned from reading the menu that this log cabin was called The Old House and was over 300 years old. It had been relocated from Beck, Missouri, better known as Arnold, Missouri, the next town over. This two-story structure was moved to its present location in 1973. It had served as a trading post, tavern, and stagecoach stop and was frequently visited by Ulysses S. Grant and his fellow officers from the military base nearby. This 18th century cabin in Kimmswick, Missouri, is worth finding for anyone in the vicinity.

As we were enjoying our dinner, the head chef, dressed in a white coat and hat, came to our table to ask if everything was to our liking. Still in awe of the place and not expecting the chef to come by, we told him it was out-of-this-world delicious!

Then our waiter came to check on us. When he found out we were boat people and traveling The Loop, he went back to the kitchen and brought back milk and eggs to us. We couldn't believe this—another kind gesture from a total stranger. He said he knew there was not any local grocery store, and he liked to help out the boaters who stopped in.

This is definitely a five-star, one-of-a-kind restaurant. It was a little expensive, but getting to walk through it to see all the Indian artifacts and enjoying the atmosphere were worth every penny. In addition, the kindness of strangers is priceless. This is a perfect place for a special occasion, and anyone in the neighborhood should stop in.

My camera stopped working while I was taking pictures outside the restaurant. This was not good! I was sick about not being able to take pictures of the rest of the trip. We were miles from any place where we could buy a camera. Being on the river system, we would be lucky if we even saw a town.

My camera was a SMC Pentex-2000, with which I could take pictures on shore from the boat (zoom lens). I was really sad; how would I be able to record the rest of the trip?

By the time we left the restaurant, it was getting really dark. I'm glad this town has streetlights so we could find our way back to the marina; fortunately, it wasn't far.

After we were back on board, Joe made coffee for morning. We relaxed while talking about our day and the wonderful dinner we had enjoyed. God has sent angels along just when we needed them; He has watched over us in so many ways.

We traveled 43 miles today and have gone a total of 3,507 miles at this point.

Friday, August 22, 2003

We stayed at Hoppie's again today. The weatherman predicts better weather tomorrow; it is supposed to be cooler. The river is down about two feet, and we were told that the next marina doesn't have enough water for us to get into it. Also, we do have electric here, and we don't know whether the next place will have it. It is still very hot and humid, and we need A/C.

Another couple, also doing the Loop, docked here, and they are worried about the water getting too low for them to travel. They have a big trawler and a much deeper draft, so they are going to try to get on down the river before the water gets any lower. They are a nice couple.

Joe changed the oil and filter while we are stopped because this marina will take the old oil and dispose of it for us.

To get off the boat for a while, we sat under the shelter out on the barge and talked with the owner's wife. She is a hard-working woman who is out in the sun all the time helping boats tie up when they come in. I imagine she has seen and heard it all being out here on the river with a bunch of fishermen coming and going all the time.

While we were talking with her, a young man and his uncle came in from fishing. They sat down and started talking with Joe and discovered they were fellow union brothers (Chrysler/GM). John, who was 34 years old, had never been married and had a naked woman tattooed on his upper arm (this could be the reason he was single). He was a fun loving kind of guy, a nice kid with a big kind heart—full of salt, as Joe would say. They had been talking for a while when John asked, "Do you need to go to the store? My truck is just right up the hill. Here are the keys. You're welcome to take it and go get whatever you need."

Joe answered, "I wouldn't want to drive your truck, and besides I don't know where anything is around here." John told him to get ready and he would take him wherever he wanted to go. Joe mentioned my camera to John, who told him there was a Wal-Mart in town about four miles away. God answered my prayers again. I got my purse and we were headed to Wal-Mart to see about getting another camera.

John dropped us off at the door and said he would wait in the truck. We couldn't find a camera like the one I had, but we got one that would get me home with some good pictures. We would see about getting mine fixed later. John had borrowed Joe's lighter a couple of times, so we bought a lighter to give to him. Then he took me to the grocery store and took Joe over to the gas station with him; we drove past the post office so I could mail some postcards. He drove us around town, introducing us to some of his friends and showing us the town's sights. He took us back to the marina, but wouldn't take any money for gas. He was a super nice guy!

I had fixed some chicken salad and fruit salad earlier for dinner. We had just finished dinner and were relaxing when John came by with a couple of his buddies and six nephews. John had promised the little boys that he would take them out skiing in his boat. It was already late, but they went out for a while anyway. When they came back by our boat, they wanted to see inside it. We invited them to come in. After all John had done for us, I wish we could have offered them cake and ice cream. They enjoyed seeing the boat, but they didn't stay very long. They were all such nice kids; it was fun to have their company. What a great day we had meeting John and his uncle and getting a new camera. This was a good day!

Saturday, August 23, 2003

We were up and gone by 7:00 a.m. because we had a big day ahead of us. We hoped we would make up some miles today going downstream. It was a beautiful day with cooler temperatures.

The Missouri side of the Mississippi has beautiful rock cliffs with a railroad going along the riverbanks. On the Illinois side there are trees and sandy beaches with wing dams every quarter mile or so. Wing dams are big piles of rocks along the shore that help control the water when it floods. Because of all the industry along here, lots of barges keep river traffic heavy.

Today on the river we saw a bald eagle, and a wild turkey was on the bank looking for its dinner. That made Joe's day.

After traveling over ten hours today and getting up to 12 miles an hour with the help of the current, we anchored in between two wing dams just short of the Ohio River. Joe was tired, but we had a good day making up some miles. We set a new record today.

We traveled 100 miles today.

145

Sunday, August 24, 2003

After a good night's rest, we got up to a beautiful crisp morning with temperatures in the 60's. The sun was up as we enjoyed our coffee while watching two fishermen in their jon boats throwing out plastic jugs with fishing lines tied to them. Then they circled back around, pulling them back up to see if they had caught anything. We never did see them take anything off the lines; they just threw the jugs back in the water. They had quite a few jugs, so it took them a while to get back around. We never did figure out exactly what they were doing. However, it gave us something different to watch while we had breakfast.

At 8:00 a.m. we pulled anchor and headed back out into the Mississippi, and at 2:15 we crossed over into the Ohio River. It was slow going on the Ohio River because we were going against the current. It seemed like we were sitting still after going so fast yesterday with all the current we had. It took us 2 hours 15 minutes to go 11 miles at about 3 mph today. We anchored at 4:30 p.m.

We traveled 69 miles today.

Monday, August 25, 2003

There was a beautiful sunrise this morning. At 7:30 a.m. we pulled anchor after spending the night listening to the big engines of tows with barges echoing across the water. They could be heard for miles; they also had huge spotlights shining back and forth across the river to make sure nothing was in their path. These lights, which illuminated the inside of the boat like sunshine, awakened me. Of course, Mr. P. didn't hear or see a thing; sometimes that can be a good thing!

It was slow going again today as we headed for the first lock on the Ohio River. At five knots against the current, we finally got to #53, the first lock on the Ohio. They were not locking through today. This lock had a wicket dam, which is a small gate used for emptying the chamber of a canal lock and for regulating the amount of water passing through a channel. They had lowered it because of the flooding through here, and we had to go over it. This was another first. WOW!

Going over the dam at about six knots, Joe looked over toward the lock office and noticed we weren't moving. A tow was coming up right behind us. We heard the tow telling the lockmaster on the marine radio that we didn't seem to be moving. The lockmaster reported back that he thought we were stuck on a pad, something on top of the wicket gate. About that time Joe added a few more RPM's to the 38 horse-powered Yanmar engine we had under us. We had no problem going on through the lock. With a tow coming in your back door, you had better be moving out of its way. Later we found out that the current was going against us at the same speed we were going (or weren't going). Just a little kick on the throttle and we were on our way to lock #52, where we had to wait 40 minutes before we could lock through.

Today we had butterflies traveling along with us, landing out on the bow of the boat. We were told that it was good luck for butterflies to land on the boat, and you can never have enough good luck. The locusts through here, though, were deafening.

At 4:00 p.m. we pulled into the Big E Marina outside Paducah, Kentucky. The marina was two barges tied together with no electric and no water; they did have fuel, which was good, because we needed to refuel. We tied up to the barge, and Joe jumped off without his shoes, not thinking about how hot the metal of the barge would be. He hopped around until I could get his shoes to him. I hadn't seen him move like that in quite a while. He was okay, but his feet got a little warm though.

After refueling, we settled in for the evening, glad for both the fuel and a secure spot for the night.

We traveled 37 miles today.

Tuesday, August 26, 2003

We were up and on our way at 7:15 a.m. Last night the temperature was down again to 65 degrees, and there was a little morning fog. It soon burned off, however, when the sun came out.

Finally we made it to the Cumberland River, but it was slow going with only 3-5 mph. We fought the current today, which made for a long day.

The Cumberland River is narrow with trees on both sides and not much else. We went 30 miles on the Cumberland and then pulled into Green Turtle Bay Marina at 5:15 p.m. after going through the Barkley lock and dam where we were raised 57 feet. On arriving at the slip, we got a pump-out and hooked up the air to cool the boat while we showered. I can't remember when we took our last shower. I thought I had died and gone to heaven and wanted to stay in the shower forever. After not showering for a while, you really appreciate a nice hot shower.

I fixed dinner on board, and we relaxed after the long day on the river.

We traveled 44 miles today.

Wednesday, August 27, 2003

We are staying here in the marina for one more night. It is a nice one with great facilities, and town is only one mile uphill.

After awakening and having our coffee, we walked to the marina's local diner, Docker's, for breakfast. This was a treat because we haven't had breakfast out for a while. After breakfast we walked over to the ship store at the marina to look around and stretch our legs. At the gift shop we asked how to get to Cypress Springs Marina. They showed us the best they could with the maps they had; this gave Joe an idea of where we were going. They were not really sure where it was.

We walked a mile uphill to town, where we found gift shops to explore. The shops, which are open just during tourist season, had some pretty items that were a bit expensive but fun to look at. Shop decorations centered on a water theme. We kept walking, passing more shops, the post office, a couple of restaurants that were a possibility for dinner, and finally a family owned IGA grocery. Everyone here is very friendly, just like home.

After returning to the boat and putting away the groceries, we walked back to the office where Joe wanted to check their maps. I went to the book exchange. I noticed a man looking at me while he talked to Joe. He introduced himself as James Taylor (not the singer); he apologized for staring and complimented me on my hair. He asked Joe about where we had been and said that he had seen our boat somewhere along the waterway. It had caught his eye because it was different looking. Without the mast, she looks totally different and nothing like a sailboat. We told him that it was very possible that after 73 stops and 3,700 miles we could have crossed paths in several places. He was a super nice fellow traveling alone on a trawler named "Sirena." His wife had just passed away, and he was headed for a visit with his family.

There were other boaters here who were also doing The Loop. After hearing some of their stories and answering their questions, we learned that there is a Loopers Club on the Internet that you can join. We will have to check it out when we get back home. Joe wasn't very impressed with paying someone to hear about our trip; he thinks they should pay him to tell them.

The couple on the boat next to ours told us they would have had someone thrown overboard by now if they had been together as long as we have been. They thought we had accomplished a great deal by getting this far. Personally, we think so too. They wished us good luck.

After all that stimulating talk, we went back to "Whoosher" to cool off in the A/C. We couldn't believe that a lot of people travel for a year, dry dock their boats, go back home to work for a while, and then go back to continue the trip. Some of them had been doing the loop for three years. That's one way to do the circle trip if you can't do it all at once, though. If I went home, I'm not sure I could get back on the boat and start again. But, then, they had bigger boats than we have. That might make a difference. MIGHT??

We called ahead to Cypress Springs Marina to make reservations for tomorrow and to find out how to get into their harbor from our present location. We wanted to make sure they have enough depth for us to get into the marina.

We walked back to town for dinner. Earlier we had heard thunder off in the distance, and we heard it again, this time with lightning. We ate at the Iron Kettle, a smorgasbord with down-home cooking. We were sitting by a big picture window eating when the thunderstorm arrived with rain so heavy that we couldn't see across the street. The power went off and we were all in the dark. Joe made ghost sounds in an effort to be entertaining. Thank goodness, the restaurant's big windows across the front provided enough light so everyone could see to eat.

The girl at the cash register was having a difficult time trying to figure everyone's bill until they reminded her everyone's dinner was the same price because of the buffet. That helped her a little. Poor girl, I think it must have been her first day on the job.

When the rain did not let up, the manager, knowing we were from the marina, had her son drive us back. We learned that the restaurant would also pick you up to do some shopping just by calling them. Many of the towns along the waterway accommodate boaters in this way because they rely on boaters for a living during the summer months. By getting a ride back to the boat, I didn't get to visit the other shops. That's one way to save money!

Thanking the young man for the ride, we hurried to get under a nearby deck to shelter us from the pouring rain. We could see our boat, but we would have gotten soaked getting to it. Finally, the rain slowed enough for us to make a run for it. Back on board, Joe made coffee for morning and we got into dry clothing to relax after an exciting day and wonderful meal. This has been a fun day.

Thursday, August 28, 2003

We were up, had our showers and morning coffee, and were untied from the dock by 7:30 a.m. After a stormy evening, the morning was beautiful with sunshine. We weren't sure what it would be like this morning, but we had a nice cool breeze as we went through the Barkley Canal over to Kentucky Lake on our way to finding Cypress Springs and Joe's friend, Ollie.

Joe found the marina without any problems (he's a good navigator). He pulled up to the docks, went to the office, and asked them if they knew Ollie. Oh yeah, they knew him all right! Joe told them that he wanted to surprise Ollie. The dock master, who also owned the marina, was eager to help Joe pull a surprise on Ollie. He called Ollie to tell him he needed some help at the marina. When Ollie arrived, he was sent down to our dock. Joe stepped out and called him by name. Ollie, who is never without words, was so surprised that he was almost speechless. He and Joe were both so thrilled to see each other again. It had been about nine years since they had seen each other after having worked together for 40 years. Ollie came aboard and stayed to talk and talk (like a couple of old women). When he left to go home, he said he would see us later and that the marine restaurant had excellent food.

We walked up to the restaurant for a very good dinner of broasted chicken, potatoes, slaw, biscuits, and pecan pie. Ollie was right about the food.

Ollie came back with his wife Joann. He had told her about "Whoosher" and she wanted to come see it for herself. They came aboard, and we gave them the five-minute tour. By the time the tour was ended, they wanted to buy her (everyone says this). After visiting on the boat for a while, they took us to their home to get us off the boat and to visit some more. These guys had a lot of catching up to do.

Relaxing on their patio was pleasant with the view of the lake just past their backyard. All kinds of birds came for snacks at the various feeders, including hummingbirds coming in for a drink. Darkness forced us inside, and the guys kept on talking; they still were catching up.

Ollie took us back to the boat after Joe convinced him that we couldn't stay at their house. Joann wasn't feeling good, and we really needed to get some things done on board. Joe made coffee for morning, and we turned in after a good day on the water and a wonderful evening visiting with Ollie and Joann.

We traveled 41 miles today. There are 1,200 more miles to go.

Friday, August 29, 2003

We stayed over to have a longer visit with Ollie; Joe enjoyed seeing him again so much. Ollie came to the marina to treat us to breakfast at the marina diner. Joann was having trouble with her eyes and also with one arm; Ollie was taking her to two doctors later in the day. We asked him to let us know what they found out.

After Joe washed down the boat, we just relaxed. Our slip is under roof and out of the direct sun so it stays cool in the boat. A thunderstorm went through this afternoon, and we could sit out in the cockpit, watching it rain and enjoying ourselves.

This evening Ollie came back to the boat and brought us a bottle of wine from Niagara Falls. He told us Joann had found out that her eye problem was the result of spraying a bee's nest earlier in the week and getting some of the chemical in her eyes. She would have surgery on her arm in a few weeks. She will be good as new when this is all done. I know she hated that she couldn't visit with us.

Joe and Ollie talked over old times until late evening. I know they were having such a good time that they didn't want the evening to end. We made plans to meet for breakfast first thing in the morning before we take off. Once again, Ollie told Joe how glad he was that we had stopped.

One interesting thing Ollie told us is that the marina where we docked is in a dry county in Kentucky, and the fuel dock just a few yards away is across the Tennessee state line in a wet county where they can sell beer from the fuel dock. That must be confusing at times—and one of the craziest things we have ever heard.

We had a good day with a dear friend. Thanks, Ollie, for the bottle of wine, for taking us out to breakfast, and especially for being a friend.

Saturday, August 30, 2003

Ollie came this morning to wish us luck and to help us push off from the docks. We promised to stay in touch and keep him posted on our whereabouts.

It was a little cloudy after yesterday's rainstorm, but the morning was cool as we headed back out to the Tennessee River that makes the Kentucky Lake. Since it is Labor Day weekend, we will have lots of boaters out on the waterway making waves. We will just take it slow and easy and try to keep Joe's blood pressure in check.

We stopped at 5:00 p.m. to anchor behind Denson's Island. So far, the thunderstorms have gone east of us. Since this is the last big weekend for boaters, they were out in full force. Other than that, we had a good day on the water.

I fixed a big chicken salad, and we ate out in the cockpit. A little rainstorm came up, which got everyone out of the lake. After that, the water calmed down for the evening. We relaxed after dinner, the gentle rain making for a cozy evening and a good night for sleeping.

We traveled 63 miles today.

Sunday, August 31, 2003

We got up to a beautiful sunny morning, had our coffee and breakfast, and pulled anchor at 7:30 a.m. Lots of boaters are already out!

We were going against a 2 mph current about half the day up the Tennessee River, so it was slow going. Getting tired, we found a nice shady spot in between two islands. We anchored behind Wolf Island about 15 miles downstream from the Pickwick Dam. Ski-dos and skiers were going all around us, so we anchored out of their way in ten feet of water, which we thought would be plenty because we need only about four feet.

The day was gorgeous with blue skies and big puffy clouds that Joe likes. We settled in, and I fixed beef and noodles with corn for supper. After supper we sponged off and relaxed before turning in for the night at 10:00 p.m. anchoring at 6:00PM we traveled 64 miles today.

The Nightmare Hit!!

"Whoosher" out of water fighting for her life!

154

At midnight (which would make it 9-1-03) on Labor Day, for some reason I woke up—call it a premonition. I couldn't get out of the bed; I thought I had had a stroke. I woke Joe up; he was over against the outside wall snoring like an old bear. Immediately he knew something was wrong. The boat was listing (leaning over to one side) about 20 degrees away from the riverbank where we had anchored.

Finally getting ourselves out of the bunk and making our way out into the galley, which was not an easy task, we called the TVA (Tennessee Valley Authority) to find out what was going on. The first question was "How did you get this number?" Joe screamed in the back of the map chart of the river from the Army Corp. of Engineer. Now where is my water? This close to the Pickwick Dam there should have been plenty of water. Needless to say Joe was upset.

Then she wanted to know if we wanted the rescue unit sent out. Joe informed her we could step off the boat and walk to the shore, that there was not enough water to float the sailboat and wanted to know where all the water was? We wanted to know what was going on.

They informed us that they quit generating water at the Pickwick Lock and Dam hydro-plant (without any notice) and would start it up at 5:00 a.m. The lady on the phone said she would call to see if she could get them to start it up sooner and get us some water. Well, that was a big joke because again she wanted to know if we wanted her to send a rescue unit to get us. Of course, that set Joe off again. He told her, "NO! I just want some water." This was not good for his blood pressure, to say the least!

They called 911 anyway, and we were called on our cell phone to see if we wanted to be rescued. Joe told them NO and that we were not leaving our boat! They said they would check back with us to see if we changed our minds. This was a clue that we weren't going to get any water any time soon.

When Joe got off the phone (thank God, we were able to use it), it was 1:30 a.m. Joe told me to get the important things I wanted to take with me and to get dressed. We had to get off the boat now before it went all the way over.

I grabbed my purse, my pictures, and camera. We grabbed a couple of boat cushions and a lifejacket out of the cockpit. Joe, being the sweetheart that he is, picked me up and carried me off the boat so I wouldn't get wet. He grabbed a rope on our way through the cockpit so he could tie the boat to a tree on shore and hopefully stop it from going all the way over. He didn't know for sure that it would even work, but it was worth trying.

We could only sit on the riverbank listening to the boat creak and hearing things falling off shelves. Little by little, it listed more and more. We hadn't been off the boat but a few minutes when I remembered that I forgot my wedding rings. I asked Joe to go back after them, but he told me he would buy me a new set. I said I didn't want new ones; I wanted mine from the boat. He climbed back on board to get them for me. I'm glad I knew right where they were. Now, that's love!

Joe had also grabbed a flashlight so we could see the boat. The rudder was completely out of the water by now, so we knew the water was still going down. We also knew it would take the water a while to reach our location if they did start to generate water as she had indicated they would.

There we sat, with our arms around each other, trying to keep warm, and praying to God that our boat wouldn't sink. Needless to say, Joe cried. He was sure we were going to lose everything we had worked on for five years, and we were so close to completing his boyhood dream.

Again and again we would hear her creak, and something else would crash to the floor. It was the most horrible feeling not to be able to do anything but sit there on the river bank and pray for the water to come back up, and to hope that it would come up before the boat sank too low to right itself. Joe walked over to check on the boat, and he saw that water was over the toe rail outside the portholes of the head (bathroom). The propeller and rudder were completely out of the water now; this was not good. This meant that she could go over at any time. Again, tears came to our eyes. We knew if the water didn't start lifting the boat back up that it was going all the way over. If water got inside, everything would be ruined. All the blood, sweat, and tears we had shed to fix her up now depended on a few feet of water.

It was getting a bit cool as we sat on the riverbank. I wished I had remembered to grab a blanket or jacket, but I wasn't going to ask Joe to go back to the boat again. It was really too dangerous now, so we just hugged each other to stay warm.

As daybreak began to lighten the sky, a young couple out fishing stopped to offer us some water and peanut butter crackers she had brought for them to snack on. We thanked them, but we weren't hungry. They asked what had happened. Then another young man stopped to talk to Joe about the situation. There was nothing anyone could do, but it was kind of strangers to be concerned for us.

At about 6:00 a.m. we noticed the water was starting to come up, but it was very slow. Joe kept wanting to get the coffee out of the boat, but I wouldn't let him go back in until the boat started to right itself and there would be no danger of his weight causing it to tip over. Finally at 9:00 a.m. I let him go back for the coffee. Oh, my, did it taste good!

We were sitting on the bank when the fire and rescue team arrived by boat to check on us. They told us that we were not the only ones in this predicament. Because it was the last big weekend of the summer, many were out boating and camping and had pulled their boats up on the shore. They were all stuck like we were except they just had little runabouts that did not require as much water to keep them afloat as our 31-foot sailboat did. We were told that the TVA made up its own rules and had caused this problem before. The TVA knew there would be a lot of boaters out with their kids on this last weekend before school starts. The rescue team called the TVA to check on the situation and found that the water should be back to full capacity by noon. They told us they would send someone back at noon to see if we needed help getting out of the mud.

Now that it was daylight, we walked the banks looking at the rocks and getting the circulation back in our legs while we waited for the water level to rise. We had been sitting on the sandy bank on cushions for five hours, but the lack of feeling in my buns made it seem a lot longer! I found some interesting rocks during our walk that I will take home with me. They looked like Indian artifacts.

Joe knew that "Whoosher" would fight for her life and re-float if we could get the water coming back soon enough. But it had to start soon. I had my fingers crossed. If the water had gotten up to her big windows on the cabin house, it would have been all over; and that's what we were praying would not happen.

At 11:00 a.m. Joe put me back on the boat. It still was not level, but there was water on both sides of the boat now and the propeller was under water as well as half of the rudder. Joe said that a lesser boat would have sunk! He was so proud of his boat at that moment, again getting teary eyed. It looked like we were on our way to getting back our home on the water. We had both prayed; thankfully, our prayers were answered.

Joe started picking things up and putting them back on the shelves. I was too frightened to move; I was just glad to be back on the boat. And there were times I didn't think I would ever say those words!

Finally we had everything up off the floor and could walk around. Then at 11:30 Joe started the engine. No problem—she started and ran like a top, but the keel was stuck down in the silt. We turned the engine off, and for once were grateful for the skiers and ski-dos going past. They would stir up the water and wash the silt away from the keel by rocking us back and forth.

At 12:30 Joe started the engine again, and she was still in the mud too deeply. We called the rescue team to send someone out our way to help us.

Then at 1:00 Joe tried again, giving her full throttle and rocking back and forth. Finally she broke herself loose from the mud and we were on our way.

WHAT A GREAT FEELING!

We quickly called the rescue team. They were glad to hear that we were floating on our own again and wished us good luck. I truly believe God's angels were in that water holding up the boat so she didn't go all the way over. It was a miracle that the boat did not sink.

When we finally were on our way safely, I checked to see if there was any water that might have leaked in. I found a little water on the floor in the head. This was the side that was down in the water at the toe rail. We are very lucky, and "thank you" prayers are going out tonight.

We headed up the Tennessee River to Pickwick Dam, where we have to go through the locks. We called ahead to get a slip at the Pickwick Landing Marina for two nights. After getting only two hours sleep, we were exhausted and we need the extra time to recoup. We pulled in at 4:15, got fuel and a pump out, took showers, and took the courtesy van to the Landing restaurant for the "all you can eat buffet." We hadn't eaten all day, and we were ready for a good meal—and a good night's sleep. That is just what we did. After eating, we called for the van, headed back to the boat, and dropped into our bed for the night.

We traveled 15.6 miles today.

Tuesday, September 2, 2003

While staying at the Pickwick Landing Marina, Joe changed the oil and filter and cleaned the water line off the topsides and deck where it had listed on its side.

I took advantage of the local grocery's pickup service to do my grocery shopping. After I finished my shopping, I did the laundry. We ordered a pizza to be delivered to the boat, and then we just did nothing!

The rain shower that went through had a relaxing sound, and we turned in early to try to catch up on lost sleep. We are still traumatized from that horrible nightmare.

Wednesday, September 3, 2003

We were up at 7:00 this morning. The sky is cloudy following last night's thunderstorms that brought heavy rain.

It was still raining as we went to the marina to take showers before leaving. At 9:00 a.m. it was still raining a little, but not enough to keep us from leaving.

We were in the Tennessee Tombigbee Waterway (Tenn-Tom) Canal. This is used by "snow birds" who migrate from the northern climates in the autumn and go back north in the spring. By using this route, mariners do not have to fight the Mississippi's current or go outside in the Gulf of Mexico. As much as 800 miles of travel distance can be saved at some points. It's a 253-mile long waterway that leaves the Tennessee River at Pickwick Lake and joins the Black Warrior River at Mobile, Alabama.

At the mile marker 437 a half dozen wild turkeys flew across in front of us to the other side of the canal. That got Joe's attention.

The first 30-mile section of the Tenn-Tom is called the Divide Cut. With high banks on both sides, this stretch of the canal took longer than any other to construct. Millions of cubic yards of dirt were removed to construct it to the first of the three locks at Bay Springs Lock and Dam. This is the highest lock encountered on the Great Circle route. The 84-foot drop is most impressive. The next two locks, E and D, are just 30-foot drops.

At 3:00 p.m. we were in Bay Springs Lake and coming upon the locks. It was still raining, but the sky had started to look good off to the west. At 4:00 we were at the dam and were being lowered 84 feet; it took 26 minutes to get through. We learned it is now called the Jamie Whitten Lock, where we were 330 feet above sea level.

Having gotten through the locks, we entered the next section of the Tennessee Tombigbee Waterway called the Canal Section. As we went through the last lock, the sky looked threatening, and we could hear thunder and see lightning. We headed for the Midway Marina.

It was getting late, so I called ahead to be sure there was a vacant slip we could get into. We were told to come ahead, and they would be watching for us with flashlights to help us into the channel that leads into the marina. We were to call them again when we got close.

It was almost dark when we got to the marina at 7:45. It was tricky getting in, but they guided us. We were told to go around the big boat and pull up to the fuel dock for the night. We broke off the air conditioner fitting getting into the fuel dock. Joe was not happy about that because we can't use the air until it is fixed (a real bummer). All in all, we had a good day. The phone is back on roaming, so we can't call anyone.

We traveled 64.7 miles today.

Thursday, September 4, 2003

We stayed at Midway today and ordered the A/C part from the marina store. It should be in tomorrow at noon. Joe put the old one back in for a temporary fix so we could get some relief from the heat.

We were told that the big boat we were told to go around last night belonged to actress Raquel Welsh and her husband. We saw a woman from the boat walking along the docks feeding the catfish this morning, but we never thought about having a movie star as a neighbor. I'm sure they didn't want it known so they could just be one of us for a change. They left this morning without any fuss.

While walking around the marina, we met some interesting people. Most are friendly and love to talk; they come from all walks of life. Many people live on boats and never leave the marina. Some come to their boats on the weekends to relax. I can understand that; there's something soothing about the lapping of the water against the shore or your boat. Some people like being close to the water.

Later we walked up the hill to the Waterfront Restaurant and had their chicken liver dinner. I would recommend it.

This marina is family owned. It is a good stop, nothing fancy, but with all the necessities. Besides the shower room, there is a front room with a big table holding a jigsaw puzzle to work if you like doing that. You can just add a piece while going through, or you can get a cup of coffee and sit there and work all you want on it. It's a good way to meet the other boaters in the marina. I like it when we can walk around the docks and talk to other boaters. It's just amazing who lives on boats and the pets they have.

WE HAD A VERY GOOD DAY.

Friday, September 5, 2003

After coffee this morning, we waited till noon to go over to the parts store to get the A/C part we ordered. When we got there, we discovered the wrong fitting had been sent.

We decided we could use the broken part for the time being if necessary, so we left Midway Marina at 12:20 p.m. We had to go through three more locks: C, B, and A. Since we had gotten a late start, we hoped to make up some time. We enjoyed a beautiful day with blue sky all around us. We are down to 190 feet above sea level.

It was late when we anchored in 12.6 feet of water in the Old Tombigbee Channel north of Aberdeen Lock and Dam. This was our first time anchoring out since we almost lost the boat. Being a bit paranoid, I'm still nervous when I think about waking up without sufficient water under us.

Joe tried to light the oven to warm up dinner, and it caught fire. We didn't know there was a leak in the shutoff to the oven. He had to use both the fire extinguisher and my rubber flip-flops that were nearby to beat out the flames on the rug. Little round burn marks were left on the rug. This made a big mess in the galley that will have to be cleaned up when we get to the next marina. We ended up warming dinner in a pan on top of the stove.

We traveled 39.9 miles today.

Saturday, September 6, 2003

At 8:00 a.m. we went through the Aberdeen Lock and Dam. We were anchored just outside it last night. Joe, who always has an idea going in his head, tried to figure out a way to take an old abandoned railroad bridge, which he saw, back to the farm with him.

I asked Joe where all the wildlife was because I hadn't seen any for a while. Looking up toward the bank, I saw two does standing on it watching us go past.

We are now in the River Section where the Tenn-Tom follows the original Tombigbee River for about 150 miles to the junction of the Black Warrior at Demopolis, Alabama. We have seen a few homes and campsites along here, but mostly we saw only wilderness along the rivers.

The original river crossed our path every now and then, making it interesting to navigate. The river went one way, and the new cut went another. The question was which way to go? This is the reason we ordered those map books back in Michigan City. The river was really not terribly difficult; but if there is a question, it is helpful to have something to check for information. It is helpful that mile markers are posted on trees or posts, but not knowing exactly where to find them (high in a tree or low on a post) keeps you on your toes as you look for them.

Transients (persons passing through) going through the locks here do not have to wait for the lock's posted times. They are permitted to go through whenever they get to the lock. This is good; otherwise there could be a lengthy wait that could put you behind for the day.

We anchored just short of Marina Cove in Carrollton, Alabama, in the old Tombigbee River. Stopping a little early at 3:30 p.m., we found a nice spot where we sat out in the cockpit and relaxed a while before starting dinner and making coffee for morning. It was nice to turn off the engine, enjoy the quiet, relax, and talk about the day. Now, this is boating!

We traveled 52.9 miles today.

Sunday, September 7, 2003

I didn't sleep very well last night. Getting up at 6:15 a.m., I had coffee, went back to bed, and got up again at 9:30 feeling much better. We pulled anchor at 10:00 and headed for Marina Cove.

We got into our slip and secured the boat. My brother Bob and a lady friend were in the parking lot honking at us. Anxious to see them, we hurried over to them. Bob brought us the blue chip that we had ordered and requested be sent to him at his address. He also brought Cotton, my cat, so I could see him. However, Cotton wasn't all that excited to see us. I think he's upset with us for leaving him behind. He ignored us and sat with Bob's lady friend. They couldn't stay very long because they had to get back to pick up her little girl. We appreciated their bringing us the blue chip for the GPS and bringing Cotton. We wish they could have stayed longer.

Soon after they left, Joe cleaned the boat and I took a nap. After going to the office and showering, we asked about using the courtesy car to go to town for dinner. At a restaurant called Down Yonder we ordered the special of BBQ ribs, baked beans, fries, Texas toast, and delicious sweet iced tea. My goodness, it was good!

All along this section of the waterway we have noticed big clumps of plant life floating in the water, sometimes even blocking the whole waterway. A few times we had to break through it. It has a purple flower that resembles the hyacinth. Joe picked a bouquet of them for me from the dock. They don't have the fragrance of the land hyacinth, but they are very pretty. The locals don't like this plant because it's taking over the waterway and clogs the water intakes of boats. It is a real nuisance to the boaters because it is everywhere. It is pretty, but not when it clogs the water system of a boat. This has been another good day.

We traveled 2.7 miles today.

Monday, September 8, 2003

Because of a dense fog, we had a late start this morning. It was 9:00 a.m. when we started out of the cove. We like to get started by 7:00, so this put us a little behind. At this point, we were one mile from the Tom Bevill Lock and Dam, one of two we will go through today.

We lucked out; we got in the lock right away. We made really good time getting through it and were on our way by 9:45. It was 41 miles to the next lock, where we arrived at 3:00 p.m.

When we arrived at the lock, a tow had blocked the lock entrance. Pulling over and shutting off our engine, we waited to see what was going on and found out that the crew was getting in its food supply from the local town. Two pickups and a van loaded with food had to be unloaded; captains were also changed at this stop. So, one and one-half hours later we were locked through. At 4:30 we were looking for an anchorage for the night.

Here we were 73 feet above sea level and headed south. We saw two deer running along the riverbanks. We have also been seeing many herons and kingfishers. At 5:30 we saw two black bears running along

165

the river, getting a drink until they saw us coming. Looking out at the bank all day gets a bit boring, so it was a treat to see the wildlife today.

We anchored at 6:15 p.m. outside the channel at mile marker 251.3. It was a warm day and also a good day on the water.

We traveled 54.7 miles today.

Tuesday, September 9, 2003

We pulled anchor at 7:20 a.m. The morning was cool and quiet. The absence of river traffic had made it a perfect night for sleeping.

Joe had heard over the radio that a southbound tow was coming, so we quickly pulled anchor in order to get in front of it. By doing this, we wouldn't have to fight the turbulence from their big propellers for the next several miles. Then we caught up with another tow about five miles from our destination of Demopolis, Alabama. This slowed us down a little because it's difficult for us to get around them.

We pulled into the Demopolis Yacht Basin at 12:20 p.m. and filled up with diesel, got a pump out, and found a slip for the night. A friendly lady with a cute southern accent runs the fuel dock here. It is always nice to get to a marina after anchoring out for a few nights.

After tying up the boat in the slip at the dock, we went for showers. What a great feeling after a few days without one! We walked over to the ship store, looking for a through hull to replace the one we broke back at Midway Marina. While walking, we discovered a restaurant that looked promising. Continuing our walk but finding nothing we needed, we returned to the restaurant where I had grilled shrimp, rice, and vegetables; Joe had shrimp and catfish, baked potato, and slaw. The food choices, and the sweet iced tea, were excellent!

The marina has a courtesy car, which we signed up to use later this evening. While we were at the ship store, we met Les and Julie, a couple on a big powerful Catamaran. They had just come from the direction we are headed, and Joe questioned Les about the Gulf. They invited us over to look at their charts. We said we would stop in when we returned from town. I was anxious to see their boat, which looked luxurious through and through.

In town we bought groceries and had prescriptions filled. When we had put everything away, we walked down the dock to Les and Julie's Cat. The boat had two staterooms, a washer/dryer, full galley, and a red leather couch in the living quarters. They had sold everything, bought this boat, and were traveling the world. They had been to the Bahamas and up the east coast to Connecticut and back, but they had not done The Loop yet. They said they would like to do it someday.

We appreciated their sharing with us their knowledge about crossing the Gulf. Once again, we have met some really good folks on our Great Circle adventure. We had an enjoyable evening visiting with some nice boat people.

We traveled 35 miles today on the Black Warrior River.

Joe has changed the oil and filter. He does this every 50 hours, so it seems like he's always doing it.

We traveled 43.9 miles today.

Wednesday, September 10, 2003

We took another shower before heading out at 9:45; it's already hot and humid. This has been a very nice place to stop; everyone was very accommodating. It is three miles from the Demopolis Lock and Dam.

When we got to the lock, a tow was pulling out. We got right in and were lowered 40 feet. We are on our way to Mobile, Alabama, and should be there in four days if everything goes right. I'm praying we have good weather for crossing the Gulf of Mexico.

There was not much to photograph along this stretch of the river. There is wilderness on both sides of the river, but we haven't seen any birds. That seemed strange!

We finally found a place to anchor for the night just lee of the State Road 10 bridge abutment at mile marker 165. At 4:45 p.m. we pulled over just enough to get out of the channel. Marinas are few and far between through here, and it is difficult finding a place to anchor.

We heard dogs barking and people talking so we must not be far from civilization. We saw that someone had been fishing here and had lost his line in the trees.

We are almost back down to sea level now. We have one more lock before getting back to seawater and tide tables.

We traveled 51.2 miles today.

Thursday, September 11, 2003

After another good night's rest, we had our coffee while enjoying a nice, crisp sunny morning. I'm getting worried that I may be getting used to this way of living. Two good nights of sleep in a row? Yikes! At 8:45 we pulled anchor. We must be getting closer to Florida because we are seeing Spanish moss, cypress knees in the water, pine trees, and fewer hardwood trees. We were going 6 knots (about 7 mph), and at times it seemed like we were not even moving. At this speed, we don't scare any wildlife or miss anything on shore.

At 3:00 p.m. we stopped at Bobby's Fish Camp, which is 2.3 miles above the last lock at Coffeeville, Alabama. It was a bit early, but by the time we could get to the lock it would be dark. This stop didn't look very promising, nor did it look like anyone was camping. I wasn't sure the place was even open for business as we approached it. The dock was just a small platform with old tires tied to it. There was a restaurant up the hill, and we walked up to it to see if anyone was around. I hoped we wouldn't get shot!

The restaurant was open, and a friendly lady gave us a menu to look over. She told us they served the best and only river catfish around.

We brought the menu back to the boat after paying there to stay overnight at the dock. There was no electric or water, but it cost the same as it did back at Alton, Illinois. Remember the 5-star marina at 50 cents a foot? When you don't have any other choice, you pay the price and are glad to have something to tie up to.

We just relaxed on the boat and enjoyed sitting and talking about the day. It was a bit early for dinner; but Joe, after looking at the menu, was curious about the catfish story. We went back to the restaurant to see what they had.

Joe ordered the river cat. Susie, the waitress, brought out a 9 x 13 inch pan full of fried whole catfish, fries, and hush puppies. Then she brought out a big dish of slaw and a small plate full of sliced onion. I ordered chicken fingers, which came in the pan with the fish. We had enough food for four people!

Susie asked if there was anything else she could get for us. We told her we had plenty. Then she pulled up a chair and started telling us the history of the area and that this was the only restaurant left along here with a license to catch and serve river catfish. Joe told her that she was right—it was the best catfish he had eaten. Everything was really delicious!

The man who catches their fish was sitting at another table. He looked to be 100 years old, with no teeth, and skin wrinkled like leather. Joe talked with him and found out that he was 67 years old and had lived on the river and fished in this area all his life. When Joe told him that he was the same age, the man looked at Joe and all but called him a liar. Joe had to get his driver's license out to prove his age. He couldn't believe Joe was the same age; of course, we couldn't, either. The man had led a hard life on the river.

Susie told us that 100 years ago this area was a resort town called Bladen Springs. Tourists came from all over to their big hotels to bathe in their mineral hot springs. Now it is just a ghost town at a crossroad.

On a table there were dozens of albums full of articles and pictures from that time period that we looked through. We found them interesting because back in Indiana we have a resort town 12 miles from our hometown called West Baden. It has the same history, except West Baden is still there along with the big circular hotel. The springs have been closed to the public. We thought it fascinating that they have similarities even though they are so far apart. It ended up being an interesting stop with a very good dinner. I hope to send her some information about West Baden Springs when I get home.

We traveled 45.1 miles today.

Friday, September 12, 2003

We pulled away from Bobby's Fish Camp at 9:00 a.m., and at 10:00 we were finally through Coffeeville Lock and Dam. We went down 34 feet to sea level once again and were back with tides and tidal currents. We haven't had those since we left Troy, New York, in the canal system. There are no tides in the river, and from Pickwick Dam all the water runs down to the Gulf of Mexico.

They were working on the locks at Coffeeville, so it took us a little while to get through. We had to stop for a doe and her fawn crossing the river in front of us. We didn't want to scare them and get them separated from each other. The little fawn was barely keeping its nose above water. I was holding my breath until it got across and up on the shore.

Today we saw loads of wood chips, coal, and asphalt being pushed with tows. It's amazing how much industry still relies on the river system for transporting goods. Passing two tows loaded down, we had to crank up the RPM's a little, but we were trying to get to the anchorage before dark.

We, along with lots of fishing boats, anchored in Bates Lake at 6:15 p.m. just north of the Alabama River at mile marker 54. This was a good day.

We traveled 66 miles today. Not bad!

Saturday, September 13, 2003

Bates Lake was a good anchorage with lots of water. We noticed a row of fishing shacks at the other end of the lake. Fishing boats had come in all night; then at 5:30 a.m. they all went back out. There must have been a tournament going on. There were dozens and dozens of boats going so fast they barely touched the water. We still rocked a little even though we were anchored out of the channel.

This morning I fixed eggs for breakfast for a change. Then at 8:00 we pulled anchor to continue the journey south. We are one day away from Mobile Bay.

We stopped at 2:00 p.m. in the Mobile River in order to get a good day's rest before entering the bay, which is a big body of water with lots of boats and barge traffic. We will be ready to tackle the bay down to Mobile, Alabama. Then it's on to the big Gulf of Mexico!

At 6:00 we had a heavy rainstorm with some thunder go through. I don't like thunder and lightning while sitting out here in the water. It's a bit scary, but it didn't last long.

The shore is looking more like the south. Because of the lower sea level it is swampy along this stretch of the river. It is not suitable for building purposes and the wildlife is not visible from the river. It does, however, have its own beauty.

We were told we might have trouble at mile marker 14 with the railroad swing bridge. We were told that sometimes it is not open and we'd have to wait for the bridge tender to get there to open it. Thank goodness, it was open when we got there.

We passed mile marker 10, just past I-65 that goes to Mobile, Alabama. We have gone over 4,300 miles so far, and Florida is getting closer every mile. I'm beginning to believe we are going to make it.

I fixed a garden salad with chicken, cheese, and crackers for our dinner.

We checked the cell phone and found we had a signal just long enough to listen to the voice messages from Michael. Bless his heart, he was just checking on us. I will have to wait till we get to Mobile to call him back. I hope we have a good signal when we get there. We haven't had a signal while down in the river system. There are too many trees and no civilization to speak of. I'm sure there are not any towers out here.

Joe changed the oil and filter.

We traveled 43.9 miles today.

Sunday, September 14, 2003

We were up at 6:00 a.m. to find it partly cloudy. After a breakfast of oatmeal, we pulled anchor at 7:15 and were on our way down the Mobile River that becomes the Mobile Bay. We ran into fog, but the sun kept trying to pop through the clouds.

At 8:00 we entered Mobile Bay. Because it wasn't as far to the bay as Joe thought, we were there sooner than anticipated.

The tows were already busy moving loads back and forth across the bay and getting them lined up so the bigger tows could push them to their destinations. With boats coming in from every direction, it was slow going in this busy port.

We went under a big expansion bridge, putting us right in the middle of the industrial section. After having spent days on the river, it was like coming into Grand Central Station. Fortunately it is Sunday, or there would have been a lot more going on through here.

Getting through the upper bay, we headed to Dog River, a channel on the west side of the bay, which will take us into the Grand Mariner Marina. We saw half a dozen dolphins trying to get to the Dog River.

Joe was stressing out, and he couldn't see the channel markers. The waves were coming in right on the beam (side), making steering rough. He was ready to take a break from the wheel and to get into the marina.

We made it into the marina, which is off the main channel. We hope to find charts here to help in crossing the gulf and going across the panhandle of Florida. If we don't find them here, we can get them in town at a West Marine.

Finally we were tied up at the dock. Relaxing out in the cockpit, we had fun watching pelicans crash dive into the water. Seagulls were also making their presence known. I enjoy the sight and sounds of all the birds around the water.

HURRAH! We finally have a cell phone signal!

After cleaning up, we looked through the office supplies at the marina and found some of the charts we need. We learned that there would be entertainment on the patio later—a guy on the guitar and a girl on drums. We took advantage of this and had an enjoyable afternoon just sitting and unwinding before dinner. The entertainers took requests, doing some Garth Brooks and Jimmy Buffet tunes plus others. They harmonized together very well.

We listened to the music until the restaurant opened at 5:00 p.m. for dinner. Our dinner of Grouper with crab bisque gravy, new potatoes, salad, key lime pie for me, and ice cream for Joe was a meal fit for the Admiral and her captain.

After returning to the boat, Joe and I started calling all our friends and catching them up on our whereabouts. It has been quite a few days since we have been able to use our cell phones. Everyone was excited to hear from us, to find out where we are and how many miles we have traveled.

Tomorrow we will borrow the courtesy car to go into town to the West Marine store for the rest of the charts we need. We will have a few days to study them, which will make us feel better.

We are getting ready to start the final leg of the Great Circle. Coming down the river section was a learning experience with all the commercial barge traffic. We found out that if you work with the tow captains they will work with you. Just give them a call, and they will tell you which side they want you to pass on. One whistle means port to port (left) and two whistles starboard to starboard (right). Or you can just pull over out of the channel, let them go past, and then continue on your way. Those barges are moving heavy loads, some of which may be hazardous materials. They don't always see small craft, so it's a lot easier just to get out of their way.

We are back to tide tables and shipping lanes with those big cargo freighters again. When we crossed Moblie Bay we were back in the ICW again. The river system was easy and mostly stress free with no big freighters and just a few fishing boats to contend with. All we had to do was stay between the banks. Now we're back to the real world and those big ships.

We traveled 24.3 miles today.

Monday, September 15, 2003

We are staying one more day at the Grand Mariner Marina. We took the courtesy car to town to the West Marine store. The chart books were $120 each and we needed two more books. However, we needed only four charts from one of the books. The store manager made copies of the pages we needed so that we didn't have to buy the whole book. He also told us about some good anchorages to stop at that we didn't know about. We really appreciated the copies and the information and thanked him for his help. This is what we like about these stores; they are very helpful and accommodating to their customers.

This used up a lot of our car time, so we had to hurry through Wal-Mart for water filters and groceries. We didn't have time to get the film developed. Stopping at Taco Bell for lunch, we were reminded of the fun we had eating there with Rodger, Dee, and Lauren in Charleston. Reminiscing put smiles on both our faces.

When we returned to the boat, I did the laundry and Joe worked on the boat. We caught up on chores such as cleaning algae off the fenders and putting them away after using them to go through the locks, filling the water tank, and defrosting the refrigerator.

I went to the marina office to look through their book exchange and couldn't believe my luck in finding a book I've been trying to find for Joe. It's a hard cover of <u>Away from It All</u> by Sloan Wilson. It is boat humor about a fellow who takes off on a sailboat adventure with his wife and little girl. I don't remember who told us about it, but we were told we would enjoy it. I have been looking for it in bookstores and in the marinas where we stop. I can't believe I found it and can't wait to read it.

Walking down the dock to the restaurant, we met a young man from Madison, Indiana, who lives here on a small sailboat. Joe talked with him, and he knew where Shoals, Indiana, is because he went through Shoals driving to college in Vincennes. He got a summer job working on a tugboat and fell in love with the water. He bought a small sailboat and is living in Mobile for the time being. I think Joe saw himself with his dream of being on the water as he talked to the young man. We both enjoyed talking with him and we wished him good luck as we left him.

For dinner we had buttermilk batter shrimp, steak fries, salad, and sweet iced tea. It was mouth-watering good!

After dinner we sat and enjoyed the music some more. We walked back to the boat, made coffee, and got ready to turn in for the night. It has been a busy day, but a good day.

CHAPTER 5

GULF COAST

Tuesday, September 16, 2003

We were up at 6:30, had coffee out in the cockpit, and looked out into the Dog River. More pelicans came in this morning. Watching them glide just inches above the water is fascinating. Seagulls were crying out and waves were lapping up against the boat and the dock piling. I love the sound of the water and can see how you could fall in love with this way of living. There's a certain attraction about it if you like living like gypsies, being on the move all the time, and having no roots. But that's not for me; I miss my family and friends back home. I'm enjoying this knowing that I'll be home soon.

It was a beautiful morning; the sun made a golden glow over the clouds. We saw a shrimp boat going out to the gulf for that delicious shrimp. Fishermen came by for fuel before heading out to see what they can catch. It's a whole different way of life when you live around water.

At 8:30 we headed to the showers, got a supply of ice, and then pulled away from the dock heading for Pensacola, Florida. It was windy and right on the beam; one and two foot waves with spray came up on the windshield. After getting out of the Dog River, we had 4.5 miles to the ship channel (we are back to sharing with the big ships again).

We could see the shadows of a behemoth ship out there already. We cut through some spoils and didn't bottom out while getting over to the deeper water to set our course for the ICW on the east side of Mobile Bay. We had to alter the course two times because of shoal water, but we made it across. At 12:30 p.m. we were back in the ICW once again. We saw our first alligator just before getting to Wolf Bay, and pelicans were perched on the navigational markers. Yes, we are back to those red and green markers that Joe can't see. (It's back to work for me— job security, remember.) We didn't have the red and green markers all through the river system. Joe, with his pipe in his mouth, has started talking to himself now. I call the pipe his pacifier; he says it helps calm him (?).

At 5:00 p.m. we anchored in Big Lagoon just around the corner from Pensacola inlet along the ICW at marker 10 at Perdido Key Beach. This barrier island is rated 13th by several hundred environmental scientists for the white sand and emerald green water that surround it. It is beautiful!

The U.S. Naval Station is located close to Pensacola, and it is also the home of the Blue Angels. Jets and planes flew right over us as they practiced taking off and landing. Joe was sitting out in the cockpit when all of a sudden he yelled for me to hurry out to see something. A 40-foot Hunter sailboat (very nice), coming in at full speed, ran aground so hard that it raised the stern (back) clear out of the water. We were anchored fairly close to the shore, so we knew he was really getting into some shallow water when he passed between our boat and the shore. Then he backed up and grounded again. As we watched him, we wondered if he tore the bottom out. He finally anchored over by us. All this was certainly entertaining.

I'm glad we anchored here—thanks to the nice man at West Marine for telling us about this anchorage. The cove is breathtaking; and the sunset, which is God's watercolor in the sky, was beautiful. We turned in for the night after having a good day.

We traveled 58.4 miles today.

Wednesday, September 17, 2003

it had come in. We think he didn't know much about operating a sailboat.

At 7:15 a.m. we pulled anchor and crossed the Pensacola inlet and Pensacola Bay. The view ahead was confusing because there were a lot of channels, all coming in from different directions. It was quite a sight, but confusing. We quickly checked our compass direction from buoy to buoy. They are floats that have consecutive numbers on them, enabling you to check whether you are going in the right direction with your map.

There are shipping channels, the bay channel, and the ICW. This can get confusing. There were big ocean freighters coming in, tows pushing barges, and pleasure boats going in every direction. Then, there were the Blue Angels flying overhead. Joe couldn't hear and didn't know which way we should go. I showed him the way on the map. I am so glad we have the map and didn't try to wing it without one. It is the one they copied for us at the West Marine store. And to think that we almost didn't get it!

Joe was still stressing out. The sun was right in his face and he hadn't finished his coffee. This is when I bit my tongue and left the captain alone. Finally we found the ICW markers, and he calmed down a little.

The Pensacola Bridge was ahead. I thought we were in the right channel and going the right direction across Pensacola Bay. The East Bay was rough going. We had wind coming from the east, which made us bounce; but that is better than rolling from side to side. I don't like it when we roll; it makes me nervous.

As we passed the barrier islands, we saw that the beaches are lined with lovely homes on both sides of us and high-rise condos on our port side. We were in the middle of the bay, too far away from shore to take pictures. The white sandy beaches through here are some of the best on the gulf coast. It is simply beautiful along here.

We went through Santa Rosa Sound down to the ICW into Fort Walton. It was enchanting cruising through here. Dolphins abound, but manatees are rarely seen even though there are some here. On one side we had the Gulf Islands National Seashore with a variety of anchorages and Fort Walton, a U.S. Air Force Base that borders this area on the north. More dolphins played in the water, making big splashes. The water here is a gorgeous blue, sparkling like diamonds with the reflection of the sun.

We have gone against the wind and tide all day. This means that it has been slow with lots of spray on the bow, making steering rough and tiring.

We anchored in the Choctawhatchee Bay west of the 283 Mid-Bay Bridge at 4:45 p.m. I know Joe was tired and ready to stop to relax after having to keep such a strong grip on the wheel all day. Your arms begin to feel like a cooked noodle.

This was not a good anchorage because the wind blew from the wrong direction and kept us swinging around on the anchor all night. It was too late to find another anchorage, so we decided to tough it out.

We could see the Mid-Way Marina from our anchorage. The building, which has an ocean mural with whales and other fish painted on the side, was lit up at night. Called the Wyland Whaling Wall, it was quite an awesome sight from the water after dark.

For some reason, I had a migraine headache and had to go to bed. Joe didn't get any supper tonight.

We traveled 56.8 miles today.

Thursday, September 18, 2003

The 15 mph wind blowing in from the east kept me awake all night. Because there was no breakwater for protection, it moved us back and forth, jerking the boat around. Finally about daybreak, just when Joe was getting up, I was about to fall asleep. He told me to go back to sleep and that he was going to get us out of there. I didn't argue with him. He started the engine and followed the markers back out into the channel.

We crossed the Choctawhatchee Bay to a cut called the Grand Canyon. This cut is 20 miles of what looked like a canal with high sandy banks on both sides and pine trees on top of some rocks. These are high banks for Florida since it's mostly flat land here. About halfway through the cut we saw a very large dead alligator on the bank. We wondered what had happened to it. We saw a big sea turtle, but it went under before I could get a picture of it. Going through this area was awesome.

It has been a beautiful day to be on the water. We have gone through West Bay and Saint Andrew Bay and past Panama City.

After last night's experience, looking for a good anchorage for the night was important. At 4:00 p.m., after nine hours on the water, we found a place called Pearl Bayou back off the channel at mile marker 295. This is heaven on earth back here, except for the jets going over. We must still be in their training area. One boat pulling a skier has been back here, but he hasn't come close enough to really bother us. Other than that, it is calm and quiet.

I am getting hungry, which means that I must be feeling a little better. I fixed Ramen noodles and added a small can of chicken, peas, and carrots. With crackers, it tasted really good to my empty stomach. Today has ended up being a good day.

We traveled 62.4 miles today.

Friday, September 19, 2003

Oh, what a wonderful night's rest! Joe picked another great anchorage. Around 8:00 the jets stopped and the skier went home. We had a perfect spot for the night, quiet and private.

With the sun up and another beautiful morning ahead of us, we looked across the bayou, which looked like glimmer glass. It was so peaceful there that you just want to stay forever.

But we had to get back to reality. At 7:15 a.m. we headed for Apalachicola, Florida, where we will stop to visit Joe's family who live close by.

The jets started filling the sky with their practice flights, they are so loud. They would land and then come back up over the trees along the barrier island. Dolphins played around us this morning. It is always a pleasant surprise when they show themselves.

While steering inside, we were bitten by some flies, actually drawing blood. Thank goodness we have a screen for the companionway. We had a smooth crossing going through East Bay over to the Government Cut. We arrived at 10:30 a.m. and were making good time. The waters through here are very shallow, so we made sure that we stayed in the middle of the channel and watched the depth gauge carefully. Joe was inside steering because of the weather or those blood-sucking flies, I sat at the door to watch the depth gauge because it's out in the cockpit. The air was fresh through here, and I could step out quickly to take pictures if there was something interesting. It was easier to watch the depth gauge also.

We went under the Highway 71 Bridge. This is the road we take going north out of Port St. Joe after visiting Joe's Uncle Paul. It's neat to go under a bridge that we have driven over!

At 1:30 p.m. we were entering Lake Wimico, Florida's most scenic lake, and from that into the Jackson River, named for Stonewall Jackson when he was governor of the territory. Then we entered the Apalachicola River that took us to Apalachicola, Florida. We have seen palm trees and were looking for manatees. They are here, but we will be lucky to see one this far north.

We arrived at Scipio Creek Marina at Apalachicola at 3:45. We had called ahead to make reservations for a few days so we can visit with Joe's

Uncle Paul and his son and daughter-in-law, Terry and Diane. Terry would love making this trip.

After settling in, we called Terry and they came right over to the marina. They live about 20 miles west of Apalachicola in Port Saint Joe. We had made arrangements to have a blue chip for Florida's west coast mailed to him and he would deliver it to us.

Uncle Paul and Terry both wanted to see the boat and were anxious to hear all about the trip. Joe had talked with them about the trip every time we had previously visited them. They had seen pictures of "Whoosher" and wanted to see her firsthand.

Coming on board, Terry immediately fell in love with the boat. He liked the pilothouse and the openness of it. Diane gets a little seasick, so she wasn't quite as in love with the boat as Terry was but she did like it.

We are docked right behind a restaurant called Papa Joe's Oyster Bar and Grill. This is what our son's friends call Joe. I will get him a shirt from here as a surprise.

We had not had dinner, so we went to Papa Joe's. Terry, Joe, and I ordered a Grouper sandwich. Diane ordered shrimp wraps, which was shrimp wrapped in bacon and deep-fried. She let me try one; it was yummy!

Joe got them all up to date about the trip. It was getting late, but because they are on Eastern Daylight Saving Time, it was later than we thought. They invited us to stay at their home so we could get off the boat for a change. We grabbed a few things from the boat, went with them, and talked till 1:00 a.m. Terry is living this trip through Joe, as are many of his friends. Terry, bless his heart, was so interested in the trip—and Joe loves to talk about it! He's so proud of himself, and they are proud of him also.

These two people have the biggest hearts when it comes to animals. They provide a foster home for the local animal shelter and help find homes for them. It's fun because we never know what they will have when we stop to visit. They are very special people.

We traveled 57.2 miles today.

Saturday, September 20, 2003

We came downstairs this morning to the great aroma of bacon, scrambled eggs, biscuits, orange juice, and coffee. We haven't had a breakfast like this since we left home. I thought I was dreaming. My goodness, it was delicious!

Uncle Paul, who is Joe's favorite uncle and the salt of the earth, came over and Joe got to tell him about our boat trip. Joe enjoys talking to him, and, of course, they all love boats and fishing. We stop to visit these good people every opportunity we have when we come from or return to Indiana.

Terry and Diane live on the Gulf; in fact, their backyard goes right down to the Gulf. They have a spectacular view from their screened-in back porch. Can't you just hear the sound of waves coming in and smell the gulf breezes? It is so relaxing here. I love stopping here and sitting on their back porch.

Diane fixed lasagna for dinner, along with a salad and bread and wine. It was delicious. It is really good for Joe to get off the boat for a while to relax and visit with them. These three guys could talk forever about boating. We thank them from the bottom of our hearts for this visit.

After dinner Uncle Paul and Terry took us back to "Whoosher" so Uncle Paul could see her. We were planning to leave in the morning to continue our trip so we had to get back to the boat.

When Uncle Paul saw the boat, he fell in love with her also, as everyone does. She has a good look for an old boat. Uncle Paul would love to make a trip like this and wants Joe to go along. I know they would have a great time together. It certainly has been an adventure for us so far.

Uncle Paul loved being on the boat. Joe showed Terry how the GPS worked with the blue chip that had a map showing your course on the screen.

After they left, we talked about how fortunate we are to have friends and family that go out of their way to show how much they care. It means a lot to us, and we hope that someday we can return their kindness.

The wind picked up just as we were going to bed, but no storms developed.

Thank you, Terry and Diane for your hospitality. We had a wonderful visit with the family.

Sunday, September 21, 2003

We enjoyed our coffee on this windy, partly cloudy morning. The weather report from the national weather computer at the office was not good. A front with high winds is coming in for at least four days. It looks like we are going to be here at least for those four days, subject to change for better or worse at any time. We could move 30 miles up the coast to Carrabelle, Florida, but there is nothing there for boaters. We decided to stay here where we are close enough to town to walk, and we can also visit with Terry and Diane.

We cleaned up and walked the few blocks to town, but not many stores are open on Sundays in these little towns. At least we get some exercise by walking. Apalachicola is a charming town with preserved historic buildings and a variety of seafood restaurants. Many of the homes are Victorian in style, and a number of the restored antebellum houses have been turned into B&B inns. The Gibson Inn is a beautiful turn-of-the-century structure located just a couple of blocks from the marina. You can watch artists capturing the casual atmosphere of the river town. An annual feature during the first week of November is the seafood festival. I would love to come back for that.

As we walked along the marina docks on our way back to the boat, we met a couple on a nice 44-foot trawler headed back to Clearwater, Florida. The captain told Joe that he was ready to leave for Tarpon Springs, but his wife wanted to wait for light and variable winds. With the storm that is coming in, the winds are not going to be light and variable for a while. Their trawler goes twice as fast as our boat, so they could make the 160 miles straight across the Gulf of Mexico up to Tarpon Springs before dark. It will take us between 22 and 26 hours at 6 or 7 knots. We wished him good luck.

When we stopped at the office to pay for another night, the owner offered us some fresh gulf shrimp he had been cooking out back of the marina. He was brought shrimp every Sunday when the shrimp boats come back in. We followed him, and he filled a container for us. We wish we had a way to take some home with us. A lot of the shrimp that we get in our supermarkets back home comes from Apalachicola. We thanked him for his generosity, went back to the boat, and savored every single shrimp. There is nothing like fresh shrimp. DELICIOUS!

The air conditioner has quit working, so Joe will have to look into that tomorrow. We can't do anything today since it is Sunday.

After that great shrimp for lunch and beef stew for dinner, we relaxed for the evening on the boat. It's still cloudy and looks like rain. Hopefully, tomorrow will be more promising.

Monday, September 22, 2003

It was a hot night without the air conditioner, so I was up and down all night. Joe got up early around 5:00 a.m. and found that it was rainy and breezy. After breakfast he started working on the air conditioner intake.

He disassembled the A/C inlet and found it full of weeds. He cleared the weeds from the raw-water strainer, which was totally clogged up. Cleaning that out fixed the air conditioner. But now we are wondering about the raw water intake for the engine. Scipio Creek was full of grass that we couldn't avoid.

The raw-water intake is located under the boat, making it really hard to reach. You have to get down in the water where we know there are alligators. We went to the office to ask about getting someone local to look at it, but the closest person was from Port Saint Joe. He arrived in a short time and checked it without pulling the boat out of the water. He decided that there must be a screen on the intake because we had traveled all this way without any trouble. He charged us $65. We hope he is right.

Terry and Diane surprised us by coming by the boat. Remember, we were to leave the next morning after they brought us back to the boat. When the weather got nasty and they hadn't heard from us, they were concerned. They called the marinas on up the ICW trying to find us. Of course, when the weather hadn't cooperated, we had stayed put. We didn't want to worry them when we found the intake problem, but we had planned to call them as soon as we had that situation taken care of.

They stayed to visit, and we decided to have lunch at a restaurant in downtown Apalachicola that advertises "The World's Largest Fish Sandwich." The fish is called Golden Tile, a northern fish like the grouper. We all ordered the sandwich with fries. When they brought our orders, we found that they weren't kidding. The sandwich was huge; there was so much fish that we couldn't find the bun. The plate was piled with fries. There was enough food for an army. There was no way we could eat it all, so we took the leftovers with us for a fish dinner tomorrow. Having leftovers is good!

Rain started falling as we walked through some downtown shops, and we headed back to the boat. Joe and Terry talked while Diane took me to the local grocery for supplies. Terry is good therapy for Joe. They have so much in common, including a love for boating.

Terry and Diane had to get back to check on the animals, but we promised to keep them posted on our whereabouts after we started moving again.

Except for the rain, we had a good day. Joe made coffee and we relaxed listening to the rain. I wrote some post cards to send to the kids.

Tuesday, September 23, 2003

The rain had stopped, but it was still windy and cloudy this morning. After breakfast we showered and walked back into town to look through the antique and gift shops. I wanted to mail my post cards. We wanted to give the weather time to clear up as was predicted so that we could take off to Carrabelle, Florida.

We checked on the weather at the marina office when we returned, and as predicted the forecast for tomorrow had changed to 10 knots with wind out of the east and two-foot or less seas in the Gulf. At 12:15 p.m. Joe started the boat, we untied, pushed off from the dock, and took off for Carrabelle. We would get a little farther across the panhandle of Florida and closer to crossing that wide stretch of the mighty Gulf over to the west coast of Florida as we begin the final leg of The Loop. With a northeast wind at 15 knots, mostly on the nose, the water was a little choppy, but not too bad. At least, we were moving and not just sitting at a dock. Joe is still a little apprehensive about crossing the Gulf.

I called Terry and Diane to tell them we were taking off and would call them when we anchored tonight. We crossed Apalachicola Bay and the Saint George Sound, two big bodies of water. Instead of going back into Carrabelle, which was about five miles northeast across the sound (we don't want to go north), we went five miles east and anchored behind the east end of Dog Island at 5:15 p.m. This saved us 10 miles of backtracking.

This is a beautiful anchorage that looks like a paradise. It's 50 miles from Saint Mark's over to Steinhatchee. We saved a few miles by anchoring behind the island. This is a huge body of water for us, especially when we are going only 6-7 knots an hour. If all goes well, hopefully we should be across before dark.

Tomorrow, ready or not, we will cross the Gulf of Mexico. The scary part is that once you are out there, if the weather changes, there's nowhere to go.

Today we rolled a little with the waves out there, but not too badly. We have 317 miles left to go on The Loop. We have gone 4,683.2 miles and 741.25 hours at this point on the trip. WOW!

We traveled 32.1 miles today.

Wednesday, September 24, 2003

We were up at 6:30 a.m. There was a slight breeze as we pulled anchor this morning. Last night the forecast on the marine radio was for two-foot seas or less. This morning it was for one- to three-foot seas, but we decided to go anyway. We got back into St. George Sound headed east into the Gulf of Mexico

Those three-foot seas were like riding a mechanical bull. We were pounding back down on the water until we were about half way (mile 36.5) across the Gulf of Mexico when it started smoothing out about 12:30 p.m. The farther we went, the nicer it got. It turned out to be an enjoyable smooth crossing the rest of the way.

Popeye, the autopilot, took over for a while after the water smoothed out. This gave the captain a chance to enjoy the crossing. We even got to see dolphins jumping out of the water. No matter how many times you see them, it's always thrilling.

We went through miles of grass floating in the water that we had to watch out for. We haven't figured out where it was all coming from out here in the middle of the Gulf, but there surely was a lot of it. We hope the water intakes don't get clogged up again.

Eight and a half hours later, after looking at nothing but sparkling blue water and bright blue sky all day, we spotted land at about 4:00 p.m. We left at 6:30 this morning, so the body's beginning to feel it.

At 6:30 p.m. we pulled into Steinhatchee, Florida, a small fishing village that supports several seafood plants. There is limited dockage space available at the marina, and homeowners will often welcome cruisers into their private docks. When we pulled into the marina, we found dock space available. With a storm coming in right behind us, we needed a place to tie up before it hit. We pulled in and docked at the first slip we came to, thinking that someone would be around in the morning.

We called Terry and Diane right away to let them know we had gotten across the Gulf of Mexico without any trouble and that we were in Steinhatchee. Joe washed the salt water off "Whoosher" while I fixed supper.

We had eaten supper and fixed morning coffee just before the rain came in about 8:00. We were sitting in the galley, glad to be in a safe harbor for the night, when we heard a loud squawking on the dock outside the boat. We looked out to see a four-foot tall bird standing on the dock beside our boat just giving us the devil. I think this slip must have been his fishing hole. He really put up a fuss. I'm going to find out what kind of bird it is.

We had a long day today, but we made it across the Gulf.

We traveled 76.8 miles today.

Thursday, September 25, 2003

This morning we awoke to heavy fog and a horrible looking sky. We didn't know whether to go or stay. The radio weather report was for 10-

15 knot winds and numerous thunderstorms all day. This is not good for boating. Tomorrow's forecast looks more promising. So here we are in Steinhatchee with no electric, no water (which means no showers), and no stores or any towns close enough to walk to.

Joe decided to take a shower in the cockpit of the boat with the hose from the fish cleaning station in front of our boat dock. He asked if I wanted to join him. I told him, " No, thank you. I will take a spit bath in the head later."

The four-foot bird I mentioned earlier is back again today, flying around, and landing on the docks around us. I went to the office to ask about it and was told that it was a true Florida heron. It stands a good four feet and has a wingspan of six feet. This was the biggest bird I'd ever seen this close, and it was very verbal.

While at the office, we learned that we actually were in Jena, Florida, and that Steinhatchee was across the Steinhatchee River from where we were. The town of Jena is too small to have its own post office. I wanted to find something with the name of Jena, Florida, on it. Our granddaughter is named Jenna, and we wanted to take her something with her name on it; but they couldn't find anything for me.

We walked to the restaurant, which was a big covered deck with one solid wall. It had a big screen TV, a jukebox, and two friendly pit bull dogs that made the rounds wanting to be petted. It wasn't yet open to serve food.

While walking back to our boat, we noticed a fellow cleaning the rusty stain off his neat old white boat called the "Jolly Rodger II." We have the same tannic acid stain on our boat. It's from the water in the ICW and very hard to get off. Whatever he was using, the stain was just melting off. We asked what it was; he told us and also told us where to find it locally. While talking to him, we found out that he is a diver and that he was born in Fort Wayne, Indiana. He moved to Florida when he was ten years old. He loved our boat; he had noticed the name and asked Joe about it. He was a very interesting fellow to talk to; Joe really enjoyed talking with him. You can learn a lot by talking to captains who have been around the water locally.

While I was fixing dinner, a big charter fishing boat came in after being out in the Gulf all day. The captain and crew got off with five other guys. We watched them unload three wheelbarrows of grouper, dolphin fish, and many more that I couldn't identify, but they were big. The marina has a big sign with its location painted on it. The sign has nails sticking out for hanging and displaying the fishermen's catch so they can take pictures before cleaning the fish. We are docked in front of the cleaning station and could see everything. After they had their fish up on display, I went out and asked if I could take a picture of all of them. They all posed with big smiles, proud of their catch for the day. They told us they were heading back to Los Angeles. I think the 7-foot guy was a ball player from the L.A. basketball team, but I couldn't get a good look at him because he stayed in the back. He had brought a crew with him from L.A. They were a nice group of guys who provided some excitement for the day.

They had just finished packing up their fish and were heading to their motor home when a storm blew through with lightning and rain.

We fixed our coffee for morning. We hope to be able to leave first thing in the morning, but it's still raining, so we will have to wait and see. The forecast for tomorrow is for ten-knot winds from the east and two-foot seas or less. We are keeping our fingers crossed.

Friday, September 26, 2003

We were up early and headed out at 6:20 a.m. with just enough light to see the channel markers. The forecast had changed to a southeast wind with one to three foot seas. We went five miles out the Steinhatchee River and then south ten miles to a marker that was missing. That really helps with navigating! Finally we were back out to the Gulf and heading south. It was a little choppy, but not unbearably so.

We were glad to be moving again and getting closer to making that young man's dream a reality. It will be nice to have our feet back on solid ground. But first things first, we have to get down the west coast of Florida.

Dolphins swam alongside the boat for quite a distance today. We saw them out in the Gulf jumping, playing around, and having a grand old time.

Going mostly southeast, we passed Cedar Key on our way to Crystal River, Florida. We headed directly into the wind that had changed to the south, making the water a bit choppy.

It was almost dark when we reached Crystal River. Going about one mile up the river, we anchored outside the channel for the night. We still had dolphins playing around the boat. The Crystal River is also the winter home for about 200 manatees (I always wonder who keeps count). The river derived its name from the clear water that comes from the 30 natural springs that feed it.

We anchored at 7:45 p.m. after going for 12 ½ hours today. I had chicken salad already made because I knew it would be late when we anchored tonight. We would be tired and ready to eat and crash.

There aren't many choices of anchorages or marinas along the west coast. It's 5-15 miles into any port, and that's based on the condition that the water is deep enough to anchor your boat. Most of them are just deep enough for small fishing boats. Also, nobody slows down for anchored boats through here.

We anchored in four feet of water with the tide coming in. Joe put out the fore and aft anchors, hoping to keep the boat from turning when the tide goes out. When we got up at 2:30 a.m. to check, the tide had gone out. The boat had turned until the anchors were so tight that it couldn't turn any more. I thought we would have to cut the rope and lose the anchors, but Joe finally pulled one out. Then we used the engine to loosen the other one. This is not something you want to do at 2:30 a.m.

We traveled 82.9 miles today.

Saturday, September 27, 2003

All night long we were treated to a constant parade of fishing boats, both commercial and pleasure. There can't be anyone left in Crystal River; everyone has gone fishing. A steady stream of boats was still going out the channel this morning.

The sky looked threatening; a big thunderstorm appeared to be coming our way. Still anchored in the channel, we were being beaten by one wake after another and were being tossed back and forth by all the water traffic. I couldn't set anything on the counters because of the waves hitting us and rocking the boat.

The fore deck was covered with grass that was sprayed over the bow as we went through that grass in the Gulf yesterday. It must be washed off before it leaves a stain. We have enough stain from the tannic acid water in the ICW without adding more.

At 10:30 a.m. I called Pete's Pier Marina in Crystal River to see if any slips are available. We were told they have room and to come on in. It took an hour to go 4 ½ miles to Kings Bay where the marina is located.

Going in, we found the channel was very narrow and shallow. Getting into the harbor, we found out that it's only four feet deep at low tide. That's cutting it close for us to float. The water was so clear that we could see the seaweed on the bottom as we came into port.

At 11:30 we pulled into the fuel dock to fill up and to get our slip location. It was beside the storage building where there was barely enough water to get around. We had to use the ropes over the piling on the dock to pull the boat to the dock. Finally getting the boat secured, we headed for the showers. We had not had a shower since Apalachicola, and it was wonderful!

Town was within walking distance, which made it convenient to catch up on the laundry and get some much-needed supplies.

The cell phone works again after not working for the past week. It will be good to check in with the kids and friends who probably are wondering where on earth we are.

I fixed spaghetti and meat sauce for dinner. Joe changed the oil and filters, as well as the fuel filters this time. It took him a while, but he had a relaxing day, which he sorely needed.

I was sitting in the cockpit when a big manatee came up behind the boat. There are tour boats here that take passengers through the cove and down the river, giving them a close look at marine life. There is even a "swim with the manatees" opportunity here.

It's a good feeling to be tied to a dock in a safe place. At 8:00 p.m. it still had not stormed, but we are a short distance from the Gulf and it could be storming out there.

We went just 5.9 miles today, only moving up the channel and into the harbor.

Sunday, September 28, 2003

After a very nice, peaceful night's sleep, we were up having our coffee and watching the tour boats and locals come into the harbor to look for manatees and to do some fishing.

The forecast still predicted thunderstorms, but the sun was shining through the clouds making a very pleasant morning. I heard church bells ringing in town, reminding me of home.

There is a small island across the bay from us that consists of mangrove trees. Egrets, small white birds akin to the heron, along with other water birds, use these trees to dry out their wings and to preen. At dusk these same birds use the trees to roost for the night. They fuss and fight for a spot, making hissing noises and squawking at each other. I wish I could have recorded the noises they made.

Joe was bored with just sitting around the boat this morning, so we showered and walked the mile to town. We ate at Wendy's, went to Big Lots, and then walked back to the boat. Joe was tired and worried about the weather; it's not cooperating. We are so close to completing his dream and he is becoming over anxious. The national weather station is predicting 4-6 foot seas and 15-knot winds out of the north, and that's not good.

We settled in for the night. Joe made coffee, and we turned in for the night at Pete's Pier in Kings Bay, Crystal River, Florida.

Monday, September 29, 2003

The wind was whipping around us this morning. The sky was overcast and looked awful. This kind of weather is predicted for the next several days and there is a small craft advisory out. So we wait!

If the big fishing boats are staying in port and not going out, then we know it's rough out in the Gulf. These big boats are losing money.

At 1:00 p.m. we walked to town. At the West Marine store I picked up The Mariner, a free magazine with loads of boats for sale and all kinds of good articles and information. Joe likes to look through it, and it will take his mind off the weather for a little while. It doesn't look like we will be moving any time soon.

While in town, we ate at the China Buffet and also picked up some groceries. We walked back to the marina, put everything away, made coffee, and settled in for the night.

The wind is whistling through here; it does not want to give up for the night. I'm glad we are not anchored out, but are instead safe at Pete's Pier.

Tuesday, September 30, 2003

We slept a little later this morning, and for breakfast we had eggs with our coffee. The sky looked better than on previous mornings; this gives us hope.

We decided to walk to town to find some pipe tobacco for Joe. Why didn't we think of this yesterday? We stopped at Wendy's and then walked to the Sheriff's Ranch store, which is like Goodwill. We found Fred's, a store like Big Lots. Its fun just looking around them to see what you can find. Sometimes you find things you haven't seen since you were a kid.

As we returned to the boat, Joe found a good bucket that someone had thrown out along the side of the road. It looked promising for future use. He never has enough containers for stuff (a guy thing).

Before returning to the boat, we paid for three more days at the office. At 6:30 p.m. a small craft advisory put out by the National Weather Channel was still in effect. This means that we are not going anywhere. To do so would be at your own risk.

As we settled in for the night, we watched the egrets come in for the night and fuss over their spots. You can see that it doesn't take much to entertain us.

Joe made the coffee for morning. I'm always stating that Joe makes coffee each evening, so here's the story about the coffee maker. We don't have a regular coffee maker, so Joe boils the water on the stove. He has a regular coffee filter holder, and he puts the coffee in a filter inside the holder. He puts the holder on top of the thermos and then pours the water in the filter very slowly, filling each thermos for the next morning, one for himself and one for me. Believe me, he has this down to a science. He makes it every night so that our coffee is ready the next morning when we get up. We can pull anchor and have coffee ready to drink. It stays hot and doesn't spill off the stovetop. Joe usually has a turkey sandwich and I have a bowl of cereal, or sometimes I fix hard-boiled eggs ahead of time. That has been our routine every morning.

If we are anchored for a few days and I have electricity, then we have something different for a change.

Wednesday, October 1, 2003

It rained all night and was still raining when we got up and had our coffee. This cloudy, damp weather reminds us of the weather we had on the east coast for a while after Rodger and Dee left us. The weather channel says it's going to change late in the week. We have crossed everything hoping they are right.

We are docked just off the side of the Kings Bay cove. All the tour boats and locals come back in here, so we can sit out on the boat and watch everyone. Tourists hope to see manatees that have come in to the warm inland waters. Here in Florida there is a fish called a mullet that jumps out of the water. We have seen them jumping everywhere back here. I think that if you were holding a net they would jump right into it. The locals smoke and eat these fish.

The water is so clear here that I could see the blue crab moving around on the bottom. Many boaters have crab pots hanging off the side of their docks in an effort to catch them.

Restless, we walked around the docks, looking at other boats docked here. We saw a neat old tug painted red, white, and blue that someone has stored here.

Crystal River is a good town to be stranded in. It's within walking distance to town with all sorts of stores, restaurants, laundry, and a bank. The weather has kept us here for six days now, and we have walked to town at least once, sometimes twice, every day. We have gotten some much needed exercise and have had a chance to catch our breath, relax, kick back, and take it easy. However, we are now ready to get going. The radio weather station is saying that Saturday looks promising for travel.

We had leftover spaghetti for supper and relaxed on the boat until bedtime.

Thursday, October 2, 2003

This morning we enjoyed that good coffee that Joe makes every night. It was still cloudy, but the sky showed some patches of blue here and there. We haven't seen blue skies for a while. The air, however, is a little cool for Florida.

We decided to catch up on the laundry and get ready to go in case we can leave Saturday. It seems to take forever to do laundry. Walking back to town again, we went to the Sheriff's Ranch store, which is like a big garage sale and fun to walk through. The $5 wool blanket we found there may come in handy if the weather stays cool. I'm sure we can use it in Indiana.

We ate at Wendy's again and walked back to the boat carrying clean clothes. As we put them away, I wondered why clean clothes take up more space than dirty ones. Joe made coffee for tomorrow morning. We noticed that the sky looks better than it has for a while. Hopefully, we will be heading south soon.

Friday, October 3, 2003

After Joe had snored all night, we were up early. By noon we had the water tank and all the water jugs filled and were going over to get a pump out. We also got ice and some snacks at the office store. We headed out the Crystal River and anchored behind Shell Island for the night. This puts us back out to the channel entrance to the Crystal River off the Gulf. We will then have just a one-mile trip back out to the Gulf rather than five miles. This is smart thinking on the captain's part! We will be on our way to Tarpon Springs soon. Our fingers are crossed that all goes well and the weather tomorrow morning will be as predicted.

A couple of boats had already anchored here; their people were having a picnic and walking around on the island. This island is a picture postcard; it is absolutely beautiful back in this cove.

So far, everything is looking good. The temperature today was in the middle 70's, sunny and beautiful with a slight breeze. Let's hope tomorrow is just as nice.

We traveled 6.2 miles.

Saturday, October 4, 2003

We were up early to find FOG! We left at 6:30 a.m., hoping the sun will burn it off. We used the GPS to get out to Crystal Bay. By 6:50 the sun had come out, but there was still a lot of fog. Hundreds of fishing boats passed us, making the water choppy and causing us to rock and roll. I was hanging on to everything so it didn't fall off the counter or spill all over me.

At 7:15 we were back out in the Gulf of Mexico—so far so good. The fog lifted as we headed out into the big water. We were about ten miles offshore and couldn't see land in any direction; the water was a light chop. The sun, a sight for sore eyes, sparkled on the water, making this a sunny, pleasant day. If only it will stay like this until we get to tonight's destination.

We saw little fish skipping across the water like pebbles being tossed across water. There must be a school of them. We were moving along, and all of a sudden one went skipping out across the water. We wondered what they are. Not very big, they shine like silver dollars, and they go for a long distance on top of the water. Joe and I made a game of seeing whose fish went the farthest. Do you think we were bored? Anyway, it was fun while the fish lasted.

At 12:30 p.m. we saw the tall chimney of the power plant at the entrance to Anclote Key. This was 25 miles away, which is 3 ½ hours for us. We re-entered the ICW at Tarpon Springs. We were so far behind schedule that we did not go into Tarpon Springs, although I wish we could have done so. Settled years ago by the Greek, it is a prominent sponge fishing area. A sponge museum is located there, and there is a Greek influence in the architecture and restaurants. I hope we can come back here sometime; there's a lot to see in Tarpon Springs.

At 3:00 p.m. we entered the ICW at the end of the Anclote Key and went on through St. Joseph Sound. It was a little choppy from all the weekend warriors, but we didn't complain. We were happy to be moving again.

We were about 150 miles from Fort Myers at that point. At 4:00 we were coming into Clearwater Harbor and were about an hour away from where we want to anchor for the night. We were getting back into civilization, and "Whoosher" got a lot of attention coming into the harbor. At 5:00 we anchored beside the Clearwater Memorial Causeway Bridge. A new bridge is being built, with lots of construction and barges around. We went back into a little cove where we anchored for the night. The only bad thing was that a lot of traffic went over this bridge.

Joe was getting tired, and we were ready to stop. After not moving for seven days and being on the water 10 ½ hours today, I'm sure his arms feel like they are about to fall off. We have had a good day.

We traveled 73 miles today.

Sunday, October 5, 2003

It turned out being a quiet restful night after all. We were up early and pulled anchor at 7:00 a.m., heading back out to Clearwater Harbor. Although it was a little overcast and foggy, it looked like we would have a great day ahead. The sun tried to wake up with a gentle breeze as we headed south.

We saw beautiful homes along the waterway where we were being passed by big cruisers giving us big wakes and knocking us around. We had to slow down or tack across the big wave of water coming at us or we would be tossed around—thanks to the inconsiderate boaters on the west coast. Other than that, we had a nice day on the water.

The water was calm and the air smelled like fish. We were going through the Narrows, a narrow canal having both condominiums and homes with canals leading to them located on both sides of the canal. The marine water patrol enforces the idle speed zone for manatees through here. Boaters were being stopped and given tickets. I'm glad someone is looking out for the manatees. They are slow moving mammals that can't be seen down in the water. Boat propellers cut into their hides and often kill them. They have been on the list of endangered species.

We saw many expensive boats as we went past St. Petersburg in Boca Ciera Bay and into Tampa Bay, another big body of water. Taking a shortcut alongside the Sunshine Skyway Bridge causeway saved us about ten miles in crossing Tampa Bay.

Up until 11:30 it had been partly cloudy, but the sun came out to warm things up fast. Even though it's October, it's still summertime in Florida.

We went through Anna Maria Sound where dolphins played all around the boat. Then we went into Sarasota Bay, Little Sarasota Bay, and Blackburn Bay to Venice.

Arriving in Venice, we anchored for the night at 5:30 p.m. in the harbor at the Venice Yacht Club. This is a nice harbor. Joe had to get around some boats on moorings, but he found us a good anchorage.

I cleaned out the refrigerator, so for dinner we are having roast beef, potatoes, gravy, corn, sliced tomatoes, cucumbers, and fruit salad for dessert.

Joe made coffee, and we relaxed a bit before turning in. It has been a good day.

We traveled 72.5 miles today.

Monday, October 6, 2003

We were up at the crack of dawn; Joe was ready to go at first light. It was a beautiful morning with the sun peeking over the trees. At 6:15 a.m. we were back in the ICW in the south end of Blackburn Bay. More beautiful homes are found along here. The canal is very narrow and reminds us of the Erie Canal.

It was very quiet; we heard only the wildlife and the sound of the water lapping on the bow as we slowly made our way through the scenic passage. It was a nice change after going through all those sounds and bays yesterday.

Leaving the Narrows, we entered Lemon Bay, a 17-mile long bay. We saw more dolphins going gracefully through the water. It was very shallow there, and we had to make sure we stayed in the middle of the channel and we watched the depth gauge carefully. It was so gorgeous and peaceful that I can see why the wildlife enjoys it back there. Dolphins were all around us, going under the boat and back and forth from one side to the other.

At 10:00 we were entering Gasparilla Sound, a large bay that goes into Charlotte Harbor in Pine Island Sound. There are fish houses back there that are primitive structures built on tall pilings for commercial fishing back in the 1800's. Fishermen would stay in them for a week harvesting mullet. Some of them were icehouses where fish was kept frozen until there was enough for a load. They are an interesting part of the history of fishermen along this part of the Florida waters. It is amazing that they are still standing, and they look like they are in reasonably good condition.

After crossing San Carlos Bay, we entered the Caloosahatchee River. The sky was full of big puffy cotton ball clouds that Joe loves so much. We haven't seen them for quite some time. Having beautiful blue water below us and a gorgeous sky above us, we had a good day to come back home. There was a good wind behind us all day until we hit the Miserable Mile at the beginning of the Caloosahatchee River, a mile stretch you have to go through before getting into the big section of the river going into Fort Myers.

We were down to 4.3 knots through there as we made our way around the little islands. We could see the Fort Myers skyline, but we were still a few miles from our destination point.

We entered a strict manatee zone that is idle speed. At 4:30 p.m. we were running out of daylight. We would like to make it back tonight to Hanson's Marina which is on the other side of Fort Myers and about two hours away by boat. It's October, and the days are getting shorter. We would have to squeeze all the daylight we could out of this day.

Getting closer to the marina, I called Mr. Hanson to ask his permission to dock at the gas dock at his marina. The marina is just across Palm Beach Boulevard from our condo, which has a nice big comfy bed in it.

At 6:20 we tied up at the gas dock (we got Mr. Hanson's okay). We had just enough light to see the pilings we tied up to. The feeling was almost overwhelming. I wasn't sure whether I wanted to jump for joy or cry.

We got a few things together and walked the half-mile over to the condo. We thought we would shower and go to a restaurant to eat, but after we showered we were so relaxed that we didn't want to get dressed to go out. We settled for a bowl of soup and some crackers, sat in our comfortable living room, pinched ourselves, and smiled from one ear to the other. Joe kept saying, "We did it! We did it!" We turned in early in our big queen size bed.

We traveled 78.6 miles today.

Tuesday, October 7, 2003

We got up early this morning, taking another shower after having our coffee. We went to the Cracker Barrel about a quarter mile away for a good morning jumpstart. We walked because the ole' blue truck wouldn't start after not being started for six months.

After a wonderful breakfast, using a gift card we received from a very thoughtful Aunt Nila before we left on the trip, we walked back over to the boat. Mr. Hanson stopped by to see us and wanted to hear all about the trip. He was kind enough to take Joe over to jumpstart the truck. Now we could unload the boat. We stopped at Taco Bell for lunch and went back to the condo to unload the truck.

Tomorrow we will take "Whoosher" back to her dock in Alva (where we started our journey April 19, 2003) for the final stretch.

Wednesday, October 8, 2003

Up early, we were anxious to get the boat back to our own dock. We had our coffee and called Greg (Joe's brother-in-law) to see if he wanted to go the last 15 miles of the boat trip with us. He jumped at the chance, and Joe went to pick him up. At 11:15 we were leaving Hanson's Marina and heading out the Orange River to the Caloosahatchee River, which makes the Okeechobee Waterway to Alva, Florida. Going through the Franklin Locks, past our canal and on down the river under the Alva bridge, we turned around in front of Greg and Mary's house, then back under the bridge and back to our canal, tying up at the dock at 1:30 p.m.

We traveled 14.6 miles today.

WE DID IT!

We can now call ourselves "Loopers" after completing The Great Circle or The Loop. We made a young man's dream an old man's reality.

This is the end of a great adventure. Thank you to everyone who kept us in your prayers.

Joe and Wyveda Philbert

We are proof that dreams can come true. Don't ever give up. The loop was Joe's dream, I'm very glad I got to help fulfill it. We now have this wonderful adventure of a lifetime to share forever.

Listing of Anchorages and Dockage's

A—Anchored out D—Docked on shore

FLORIDA

4/19 A-Moore Haven

4/20 A-Poet Mayaca

4/21 A-Manatee Pocket-Stuart

4/22 A-Jones Fruit Dock-Indian R

4/23 A-Whitley Bay Marina-Cocoa

4/24 A-Sheephead Cut-New -Smyrna

4/25 A-Cement Plant-Flagler -Beach

4/26 D-Oyster Creek Marina - St. Augustine

4/27 A-Fernandina Beach, Fl. - Bells R.

GEORGIA

4/28-29 A-Ft. Frederica-Frederica R

4/30 A-Big Tom Creek-Behind Ossabaw Is.

SOUTH CAROLINA

5/1 A-Skull Creek-Port Royal Sound
5/2 D-City Marina-Beaufort
5/3-4 D-Charleston City Marina
5/6 A-Sampit Point-Georgetown
5/7 A-Enterprise Creek
5/8 D-Barefoot Landing-Myrtle Beach

NORTH CAROLINA

5/9 D-Masonboro Boat Yard & Marina- Wilmington
5/10 A-Mile Hammock Bay-Sneads Ferry
5/12-13 D-Sea Gate Marina-Alligator R-Morehead City
5/14 D-Dowery Creek Marina-Belhaven
5/15 D-Alligator Marina-Alligator River
5/16 D-Elizabeth City Marina-Elizabeth City
5/17-18 D-No. Carolina Welcome Center-Dismal Swamp

VIRGINIA

5/19 A-Lafayette River-Outside Norfolk
5/20 A-Reedville-Wicomico River-Chesapeake Bay
5/21 Rodger and Dee left to go home.

MARYLAND

5/21 A-Mill Creek – (Outside) Solomons Is.
5/22-24 A-Solomons Islands
5/25-26 A-Lake Ogleton-Severn River-outside Annapolis
5/27 A-Chesapeake City-Chesapeake-Delaware Canal

NEW JERSEY

5/28 A-Cape May-Cold Springs
5/29 A-Back in a cove-Ventnor City
5/30-6/1 D-Beach Haven Marina
6/2 A-Gimmerglass-Crab Town Creek
6/3-5 D-Keyport Yacht Club-Keyport

NEW YORK

6/6 A-Behind Pollepel Island-Hudson River
6/7 A-Rondout Creek-Kingston
6/8 A-Behind Coxsackie Island-Hudson River
6/9-10 D-Waterford City Wall-Start of Erie Canal
6/11 D-Amsterdam City Wall-Erie Canal
6/12 D-llion City Wall
6/13-14 D-Sylvan Beach City Wall-Oneide Lake
6/15 D-Smitty Roadside Tavern along a wall on Erie
6/16 D-Brockport City Wall-Erie Canal
6/17 D-Lockport -behind lock #35
6/18-19 D-Tonawanda City Wall
6/20-22 D-Tonawanda City Wall-End of Erie Canal
6/23 A-Dunkirk-Inside breakwater-Lake Erie

OHIO-LAKE ERIE

6/24 A-Ashtabula-Harbor off Lake Erie
6/25 A-Lorain-Behind breakwater
6/26 A-Battery Park Marina-Sandusky
7/16-18 Back on boat after going home for three weeks

MICHIGAN

7/19-20 D-Erma Henderson Park &Marina-Detroit

7/21 D-South Channel Yacht Club-St. Clair River

7/22 D-Port Huron City Dock - Black River-L. Huron

7/23 D-Port Sanilac Marina - L. Huron

7/24 A-Harbor Beach- Lake Huron

7/25-26 D-Harrisville Marina-Lake Huron

7/27-28 D-Alpena Harbor Marina-Thunder Bay-L. Huron

7/29 D- Rodger's City Marina- Lake Huron

7/30-8/1 D-Mackinaw City Marina

8/2 A-Charlevoix Harbor-Lake Michigan

8/3 D-Frankfort City Marina-Lake Michigan

8/4 D-Manistee City Marina-Lake Michigan

8/5 A-Pentwater Harbor-Lake Michigan

8/6-7-8 D-Hartshorn Marina-Muskegon-L. Michigan

8/9 D-South Haven City Marina-Lake Michigan

INDIANA

8/10-11 D-Michigan City Marina-Lake Michigan

8/12-13 D-Michigan City Marina-Lake Michigan

ILLINOIS

8/14 D-Joliet City Pier-Illinois River

8/15 A-Ottawa - Behind Mayo Island -
On the Illinois River

8/16 A-Behind Sunken Barge

8/17 D-Pekin Boat Club-Illinois River

8/18 D-Beardstown Public Access Dock

8/19 A-Behind Twelve Mile Island - Illinois R.

8/20 D-Alton City Marina - Illinois R.

MISSOURI-Mississippi River

8/21-22 D-Hoppie's Marina Barge-Kimmswick
8/23 A-Cape Girardeau

ILLINOIS-Ohio River

8/24 A-Mound City

KENTUCKY

8/25 D-Big "E" Marina Barge-Paducah-Illinois R.
8/26-27 D-Green Turtle Bay Marina-Grand Rivers
8/28-29 D-New Concord- Cypress Springs Marina

TENNESSEE

8/30 A-Behind Denson Island. Mile 125
8/31 A-Behind Wolf Island-Above Pickwick Dam
9/1-2 D-Pickwick Landing Marina &State Park-Counce

MISSISSIPPI

9/3-4 D-Fulton-Midway Marina-Tim-Tom Waterway
9/5 A-Behind Island on original Tombigbee R-mile 361.5

ALABAMA

9/6 A-Aliceville Lake-above Pickensville-mile 309
9/7 D-Marina Cove-above Tom-Bevill Lock &Dam
9/8 A-Mile Marker 251.3 outside channel in river
9/9 D-Demopolis Yacht Basin
9/10 A-Behind Highway 10 Bridge - mile marker 165
9/11 D-Bobby's Fish Camp Pier-Silas-mile m. 119
9/12 A-Bates Lake off Tombigbee River-mile m. 54
9/13 A-Mobile River cut at mile m.10 outside channel
9/14-15 D-Grand Mariner Marina-Dog River-Mobile Bay

FLORIDA

9/16 A-Big Lagoon- ICW-Mile m. 10 before Gulf Breeze
9/17 A-Choctawhatchee Bay Bridge- outside channel
9/18 A-Pearl Bayou-St Andrews Bay& East Bay m.295.4
9/19-22 D-Scipio Creek Marina-Apalachicola
9/23 A-Behind Dog Island-across from Carrabelle
9/24-25 D-Gulf-Stream Motel & Marina-Jena-Steinhatchee
9/26 A-Crystal River Channel-off-Gulf-marker 24
9/27-10/2 D-Pete's Pier-Kings Bay-Crystal River
10/3 A-Behind Shell Island-Crystal R-off Gulf
10/4 A-Beside Clearwater Memorial Bridge Causeway
10/5 A-Venice Yacht Club-in Harbor
10/6-7 D-Hanson Marina Ways-Orange River
10/8 D- At our Dock in Alva

LOCKS

1. Moore Haven
2. Port Mayaca
3. St. Lucie
4. So. Mile
5. Troy, #1-Federal
6. Waterford-Erie Canal- #2-#35
7. Buffalo-Federal into Lake Erie
8. Chicago Harbor
9. Lockport
10. Brandon Road
11. Dresden
12. Marseilles
13. Starved Rock
14. Peoria
15. La Grange
16. Melvin Price-Alton, Ill.
17. Chain of Rock-Granite City, Ill.
18. Smithland-Lock #53
19. Lock #52
20. Barkley-Grand River-Ky.
21. Pickwick Hydo-Plant-Counce, Tenn.

22. Jamie Whitten-Bay Spring's, Miss.
23. Lock "E"-Sonny Montgomery-Miss.
24. Lock "D"-John Rankin-Fulton, Miss.
25. Lock "C"-Fulton
26. Lock "B"-Glover Wilkins-Miss.
27. Lock "A"-Amory, Miss.
28. Aberdeen, Miss.
29. John C. Stennis-Columbus, Miss.
30. Tom Bevill-Aliceville, Al.
31. Howell Heflin-Gainesville, Al.
32. Demopolis
33. Coffeeville
34. Franklin-Caloosahatchee River

www.ingramcontent.com/pod-product-compliance
Lightning Source LLC
Chambersburg PA
CBHW071156130626
46553CB00004B/1680